ALL AROUND
THE
TOWN

ALL AROUND THE TOWN

By Herbert Asbury

THUNDER'S MOUTH PRESS ★ NEW YORK

ALL AROUND THE TOWN

© 1929, 1930, 1931, 1932, 1933, 1934 by Alfred A. Knopf, Inc.

© 2003 by Thunder's Mouth Press

Published by
Thunder's Mouth Press
An Imprint of Avalon Publishing Group Incorporated
245 West 17th St., 11th Fl.
New York, NY 10011

Published by arrangement with Alfred A. Knopf, Inc.

Library of Congress Cataloging-in-Publication Data is available.

ISBN 1-56025-521-8

9 8 7 6 5 4 3 2 1

Designed by *Pauline Neuwirth, Neuwirth & Associates, Inc.*
Printed in the United States of America
Distributed by Publishers Group West

To Hannah S. Hahn

Author's Note

Many of the stories in this book were originally published in *The New Yorker*; two appeared in *Detective Story Magazine* and *The New York Herald Tribune*. Several, however, are here published for the first time. The material on which they are based came from standard historical works of reference, from newspapers and magazines, and from various official records. Some of the incidents described are referred to in my previous books on New York— *Ye Olde Fire Laddies* and *The Gangs of New York*, but are here presented in greater detail.

H. A.

Beverly Hills
California
September 15, 1934

CONTENTS

LIST OF ILLUSTRATIONS

ALL AROUND
THE
TOWN

CHAPTER 1

THE ECCENTRIC CORNBURYS

ON MAY 3, 1702, Edward Hyde, Lord Cornbury, eldest son of the Earl of Clarendon and first cousin to Queen Anne of England, to whom he bore an extraordinary facial resemblance, arrived in New York to become His High Mightiness the Governor of the Colony—a resounding title employed by the Dutch governors and retained for some fifty years by their English successors. He was accompanied to the New World by Lady Cornbury, who was a granddaughter of the Earl of Richmond. They landed at the Battery with much fuss and ceremony, while guns boomed from the battlements of the Fort, and the assembled populace greeted them with loud and enthusiastic huzzas. Lord Cornbury's reputation in London had been that of a fop and a wastrel, but he was known to be high in the favor of his royal kinswoman, and the loyal colonists were confident that he would be able to remedy some of the many abuses which had been heaped upon them by his predecessors.

In the first flush of fervent welcome the city authorities voted Lord Cornbury two thousand pounds to defray the expenses of his voyage from England. The money was presented to him at a formal banquet attended by the leading citizens, including members of such famous colonial families as the Van Cortlandts, the De Peysters, and the Van Rensselaers. His High Mightiness had announced that he would address his subjects at the conclusion of the feasting, and the colonists expected him to outline his policies and tell them what sort of government they might hope for during his administration. Instead, he delivered a rhapsodic eulogy of Lady Cornbury's ears, which he described in flowery language as the most beautiful in Christendom. He required every gentleman present to march past and feel for himself their shell-like texture. This embarrassing task was at length completed to the satisfaction of His High Mightiness, and the leading citizens went home slightly bewildered. They were even more perplexed a week or so later when the Governor and Lady Cornbury gave a grand ball at the gubernatorial mansion in the Fort and compelled the guests to pay admission. Several who had been invited failed to appear at the function, and His High Mightiness said angrily that he would ask the colonial assembly to levy a special tax on them and force them to pay his admittance fee. However, if he ever did make such an extraordinary request, there is no record of it.

These exploits were the first of a long series of eccentricities in which Lord and Lady Cornbury apparently strove to outdo each other. The staid citizens of New York had scarcely ceased talking about the Governor's ball when he scandalized them anew by riding his horse up the steps and through the doorway of the King's Arms Tavern, on the west side of Broadway just north of the English Church, as Trinity was then called. His High Mightiness spurred his steed to the bar and ordered the landlord to bring drink—whisky for himself and water for his beast. Then he clattered out, smashing a few chairs and tables as he went.

A few nights later the night watchman was amazed to see a feminine figure prancing along the ramparts of the Fort, coyly calling the colonial equivalent of "Yoohoo!" Brandishing his staff, the watchman rushed forward to take the obviously tipsy lady into custody, but he had no sooner seized her than she flung her arms around his neck and began pulling at his ears, which were decidedly not shell-like in texture. The gleam of the watchman's lanthorn fell upon the industrious figure, and imagine his surprise and horror to discover that the supposed inebriated female was none other than His High Mightiness, the Governor of New York, becomingly clad in Lady Cornbury's best silks and satins, both mentionables and unmentionables! The watchman fought fiercely, preserved his honor and gained his freedom, and fled into the night, while Lord Cornbury, shrieking and giggling, danced gayly back into the Fort.

Thereafter, two or three times a week, but always at night, His High Mightiness appeared on the streets of New York wearing Lady Cornbury's clothing. He was invariably drunk and disorderly, but he was not molested, for the night watchman realized that to interfere with the Governor's little outings would imperil his job, and probably his liberty as well. It was the embarrassing custom of His High Mightiness to

Lord Cornbury

hide behind a tree, and from this shelter pounce upon a belated pedestrian and rapturously pull his ears.

Criticism of these curious antics inevitably came to the knowledge of Lord Cornbury, and in order, as he said, to still the lying tongues of malicious gossips, he made several explanations of his penchant for dressing as a woman. He said first that since he resembled Queen Anne to such a remarkable degree, he occasionally donned skirts and paraded the streets solely that he might acquaint the colonists with the appearance of their sovereign, whom none of them would probably ever see. This explanation didn't seem to satisfy anybody, so His High Mightiness said that he sometimes dressed as a woman simply because he was the New World representative of the Queen, and he thought that the people should be reminded from time to time that they were ruled by a woman. Colonial eyebrows were still lifted, so Lord Cornbury finally announced with considerable dignity that he had made a vow which compelled him to wear dresses one month each year. And if that wasn't sufficient for the citizens, he implied, they could concoct a few explanations of their own.

Curiously enough, or perhaps not so curiously, Lord Cornbury was a devout church member and never neglected his religious duties. One of his peculiarities, or eccentricities, was an intense hatred of Presbyterians, with a corresponding affection for Episcopalians. During an epidemic of smallpox and yellow fever in New York in 1703, he fled with his family to the little village of Jamaica, on Long Island, where the Presbyterians offered him the use of their new parsonage, no other house in the town being thought fine enough for His High Mightiness. The Governor occupied the parsonage for a few weeks, and then gave it to the Episcopalians, together with all the farm land near Jamaica owned by the Presbyterian organization. Encouraged by this display of generosity, several Episcopalians obtained, through trickery, the keys to the Presbyterian church and took possession of it on a Sabbath afternoon. Next day the Presbyterians tried to recapture their building, and after considerable hard fighting forced their way inside, where they ripped up the seats and otherwise damaged the interior. Lord Cornbury sent his personal servants to help the Episcopalians, and the Presbyterians were driven from the building. His High Mightiness then ordered the Presbyterians prosecuted for damaging the church, and several were fined or imprisoned. It was not until 1728, a quarter of a century later, that the colonial courts finally restored the property to the Presbyterians.

Lord Cornbury's creditors were barking at his heels when he left England, and he continued to be hard pressed for money all the time he was Governor of New York. He borrowed from everyone who would lend him a shilling, and raised money in a great variety of dishonest ways, sometimes even brazenly stealing from the public funds. One of his most prolific sources of revenue was the sale of public lands, vast acreages of which were granted to his friends and loyal henchmen for ridiculously small sums. He was supposed to transfer this money to the public treasury, but he never did so, and always refused to make an accounting. One of the most brazen of these steals gave several thousand acres north of Poughkeepsie, along the Hudson River, to nine men, one of whom was secretary to His High Mightiness. In honor of Lord Cornbury they named the grant Hyde Park.

An Englishman named Isaac Bedlow, who had made a fortune in the East Indies, came to New York while Lord Cornbury was Governor, and received from His High Mightiness a contract to provision the English fleet. Bedlow bought an island in the harbor (it is still called by his name, with a slight change in spelling), on which he stored a great quantity of foodstuffs for delivery to the warships. Soon thereafter he died suddenly, and Lord Cornbury took charge of his papers. Extracting the vouchers which had been issued for the provisions, he cashed them at the colonial treasury and pocketed the money. So far as the records show, he never made restitution to Bedlow's widow and children, who were reduced to actual want.

About a year after Lord Cornbury's arrival in New York a French privateer appeared off Sandy Hook and began firing guns and otherwise terrorizing the shipping. His High Mightiness called a special session of the colonial assembly, which convened on April 8, 1703. He told the statesmen that he had received private information that a French fleet was sailing northward along the Atlantic coast to attack the city, and requested an appropriation of fifteen hundred pounds with which to erect a battery of guns on each side of the Narrows. In great excitement the legislators levied a special poll tax upon lawyers, bachelors, citizens who wore periwigs (they were worn only by the aristocrats and men of substance), and other unfortunates. The money thus raised was turned over to Lord Cornbury, but instead of building fortifications he constructed a pleasure house for his own use on Governors Island, which had been the playground of the rulers of the colony since 1637, when Governor Van Twiller bought it from the Indians for a few nails, a string of beads, and two ax-heads. Only brief references to Lord Cornbury's pleasure house can be found in the standard histories of New York, and perhaps the less said about it the better. Certainly the noble lord's pleasures appear to have been of a sort scarcely to be expected of a High Mightiness. His misappropriation of the colony's armament funds caused much indignation, but Lord Cornbury confounded his critics by pointing out, with unanswerable logic, that since the expected attack had not materialized, the purpose of the appropriation had been accomplished. Therefore, what did it matter how the money had finally been expended?

Lady Cornbury's eccentricities were not quite so spectacular as those of His High Mightiness, but they were scarcely less objectionable to the colonists. As soon as she had settled herself in the Governor's Mansion, the principal ladies of the city called to pay their respects, and to their surprise, for they were naturally suspicious of a lady who had compelled them to pay admission to her party, they were graciously received.

Lady Cornbury announced that she intended to maintain a court as similar as possible to the court of Queen Anne in London, and that she would select six young women from the colony's most important families to live at the Mansion and act as her maids-of-honor. There was much rivalry for this distinction, and the six who were at length chosen were regarded as having been greatly honored. When the fortunate six arrived at the Governor's Mansion, however, Lady Cornbury immediately discharged her domestic servants, and the maids-of-honor were put to work in the kitchen and as chambermaids. They protested, but, at the request of Lady Cornbury, His High Mightiness posted a guard of soldiers about the Mansion, and the young ladies were threatened with imprisonment and the lash unless they cheerfully cooked, washed the dishes, and made the beds. They were not permitted to leave the Mansion until their irate parents came and virtually took them by force.

The only coach in New York was owned by Lady Cornbury, and one of her greatest pleasures was to ride abroad on rainy days and splash mud and water upon less fortunate ladies who were compelled to walk. Two or three times a week she toured the city in her grand equipage, and entered any house that attracted her attention. Once inside, she carefully surveyed the premises, and if anything struck her fancy, she ordered it placed in her carriage and taken to the Governor's Mansion. Next day she sent word to the owner of the article that she had tired of it, and that unless he redeemed his property by paying a sum greatly in excess of its worth, she would sell it as junk. Several families were compelled to buy their own china, lace, and other belongings from peddlers to whom Her Ladyship had sold them.

This noble creature tormented the colonists until August 11, 1706, when she died at the age of thirty-four and was buried in Trinity churchyard. With characteristic patience, which has not lessened with the passage of years, New York put up with Lord Cornbury for two years longer, when his conduct finally became so outrageous that the leading citizens sent petitions to London demanding the appointment of a new governor.

Lord Cornbury was removed from office in 1708. He attempted to sail secretly for Europe, but before he could board the ship, his creditors stormed the Governor's Mansion and raised such a furor that the deposed High Mightiness was lodged in debtors' prison. There he remained for several months, until his father died and he became the Earl of Clarendon. Money from the estate in England paid the most pressing of his debts, and without fuss or ceremony he sailed for London, and so passed from the pages of American history.

CHAPTER 2

FORTY DAYS AND FORTY NIGHTS

THE FIRST time New York ever heard of Dr. Henry S. Tanner was during the late spring of 1880, when a brief dispatch to the *Times* from Hudson, Wisconsin, identified him as a graduate of the Eclectical Medical Institute of Cincinnati (class of 1859), who had abandoned medicine for the lecture platform and had acquired a wide reputation in the Northwest as an implacable foe of tea, coffee, tobacco, and liquor. The meat of the dispatch, however, was a statement by Mrs. Tanner, whom the *Times'* correspondent described as "of nervous-bilious temperament, cultured mind, and a good feeder," that she was leaving the doctor forthwith because he wouldn't let her have enough to eat. To this, Dr. Tanner replied that his wife was such a gross eater that she made him downright ill, and that he hoped by withholding food to rescue her from the sin of gluttony. Next day the *Times* quoted the indignant lady as saying that her husband apparently expected her to live on air, whereupon Dr. Tanner retorted that air—plus a little water and an occasional crust—was quite enough. Everyone, he declared, ate too much and would be greatly benefited by frequent fasts. He had tested his theory, he said, and in 1877, while living in Minneapolis, had fasted forty-two days, from July 17 to August 29, thereby curing himself of asthma, rheumatism, and heart disease. He admitted that this feat had been performed in the privacy of his home, without supervision.

Important news being scarce in New York—the time was a year before the assassination of President Garfield and three years before the opening of Brooklyn Bridge—the other newspapers became interested in the controversy, which was destined so to develop as to make Dr. Tanner, for a few months, the most talked-about man in the world. Moreover, it set the medical profession by the ears and precipitated a bitter wrangle between the allopathic and the eclectic physicians. Dr. Tanner had been an eclectic before he retired from active practice, and he was still fiercely loyal to his medical brethren. The uproar between the two schools of medical doctrine became so furious that poor Mrs. Tanner was soon forgotten, despite an occasional plaintive dispatch from Wisconsin that she was still hungry. The sole question at issue, after the first week or so, was how long Dr. Tanner could abstain from food without starving.

The New York *Herald* asked the opinion of Dr. William H. Hammond, formerly Surgeon-General of the United States Army, and one of the city's leading physicians, who said flatly that Dr. Tanner's statements were bosh. In reply Dr. Tanner simply pointed out that Dr. Hammond was an allopath, and intimated that to an allopath everything might very well be bosh. To prove the correctness of his theory, he offered to fast for forty days and forty nights, under strict supervision, for five thousand dollars, of which he promised to give four thousand to charity. Dr. Hammond said that was more bosh, whereupon Dr. Tanner declared that a fast of forty days would be child's play for him because he was born in Tunbridge Wells, Kent, England, and had lived there for seventeen years.

No one saw the significance of his birthplace until Dr. Tanner explained that he had drunk so copiously of the chalybeate waters of the Tunbridge Wells that the inner lining of his stomach had acquired a permanent coating of iron salts, which provided him with a source of inner nourishment. The doctors were greatly excited by this statement. Several suggested that Dr. Tanner make provisions in his will for a postmortem examination by a committee of reputable surgeons; and one wanted to cut a hole in his stomach at once and peek. Dr. Tanner refused to undergo such an operation, on the ground that it would impair his usefulness for too long a period. Also, he feared that it might start a leak in his iron salts deposit.

Dr. Hammond informed the newspapers that all this was the worst bosh he had ever heard, that Dr. Tanner was obviously crazy, and that he washed his hands of the whole affair. The *Times* was inclined to agree with his estimate of Dr. Tanner's mental condition, remarking editorially that the latter's "offer to undergo this extraordinary test was *prima facie* evidence that he was either a fraud or a lunatic." But the eclectic physicians of New York rushed to Dr. Tanner's defense,

Dr. Tanner in the Second Week of His Fast

and late in June 1880 announced that their hero would come to the metropolis and fast in public under the supervision of the United States Medical College, an eclectic institution, which would provide a corps of watchers headed by Dr. Robert A. Gunn, Dean of the College and Professor of Surgery.

The New York Neurological Society, composed of allopaths, promptly notified the newspapers that it would also have watchers at the scene of the fasting, and intimated that they would be instructed to watch the eclectic watchers as well as Dr. Tanner. And the New York *Herald,* with a great burst of editorial pride, announced that if Dr. Tanner survived the first week, it would assign reporters, and doctors who belonged to neither of the warring factions, to maintain a constant watch over everybody for the remainder of the fast. The *Herald* pointed out that this bit of journalistic enterprise would cost them seventeen hundred dollars, assuming that Dr. Tanner lived the full forty days.

On behalf of the intrepid faster, Dr. Gunn and his associates engaged Clarendon Hall in West Thirteenth Street. At the rear of the auditorium a space forty-five feet long and thirty-five feet wide was railed off and equipped with a rocking chair, an iron cot and mattress, and a writing-stand. Outside the railing were long tables for the watchers and reporters. The remainder of the hall was for the use of the general public, and everybody was invited to come and watch Dr. Tanner do without food.

About half past eleven o'clock on the morning of June 28, 1880 Dr. Gunn and the first shift of watchers from the Medical College and the Neurological Society entered the hall, accompanied by Dr. Tanner, who was a short, roly-poly little man with sparse gray hair. He was wildly cheered by the several hundred persons who had crowded into the hall, and by an even greater number who waited impatiently outside the building for word that the great experiment had begun. Ladies in the audience were invited to turn their heads, and Dr. Tanner was stripped and carefully searched, to make certain that no food was concealed on his person or in his clothing. He was then weighed, and it was solemnly noted that he tipped the beam at 157½ pounds. He was fifty-one years old.

A few minutes before twelve o'clock Dr. Tanner, having resumed his clothing, was escorted into the railed-off enclosure by Dr. Gunn and Dr. Edward Bradley, chief of the Neurological Society's watchers, and at noon exactly Dr. Gunn blew a whistle. He and Dr. Bradley then bowed and retired to the watchers' tables, while Dr. Tanner sighed, scratched his head, and sank into his rocking-chair. At one minute past noon he began rocking vigorously, and the watchers settled down to serious watching. They worked in six-hour shifts, and from six to ten were constantly on duty.

Thus did Dr. Tanner begin his fast, which is still reckoned as one of the most extraordinary stunts New York has ever seen. From the beginning it attracted great attention, and in the eastern part of the United States it was nothing less than a sensation. Physicians from other cities made long journeys to watch the faster for an hour or two; ministers preached sermons denouncing Dr. Tanner for meddling with the heavenly laws of hunger and appetite; and every day and most of every night Clarendon Hall was crowded with visitors, who stood patiently, as the *Herald* put it, "watching Dr. Tanner not eat." Admittance was free for the first ten days, but after that twenty-five cents was charged.

To the newspapers the fast was manna from Heaven; they printed news stories by the page and editorials by the column, besides special articles signed by physicians and other authorities. So far as making the most of such an opportunity was concerned, however, New York journalism was still in its infancy; apparently it occurred to no editor to publish an account of Dr. Tanner's life and loves. The *Times* changed its mind about the faster, and after describing the fast as "one of the most curious experiments, from a physiological point of view, ever seen in the city," it said that "the expression of his face is intelligent, and a moment's conversation with him will undeceive any person who imagines him to be a fool."

As a natural result of the publicity given his feat, Dr. Tanner received innumerable gifts, including a great variety of patent beds and music boxes, while his fan mail was never less than three hundred letters a day, and sometimes was as much as five hundred. Some of the writers devoted themselves to tormenting the doctor with rhapsodic descriptions of Lucullan feasts, others urged him to quit lest God strike him dead, and many expressed the idea embodied in this letter from J. F. Snipes of Staunton, Virginia, which Dr. Tanner received on July 13:

"Dr. Tanner:—Please do not succeed. If you do you will shock the orthodox, not only of the M.D.'s, but of those who doctor divinity. If the miracle of fasting forty days (and nights) unwatched, in the wilderness (Matt. 4:2), be true and an evidence of divinity, will you be any less divine if you do the same thing?"

Throughout the fast there was almost constant bickering between the Medical College watchers and those from the Neurological Society, the latter maintaining that the eclectics were systematically feeding Dr. Tanner in some manner which they could not detect, although no proof of this was ever forthcoming. The only really serious dispute between the warring factions, however, occurred at midnight on the tenth day of the fast, when Dr. Bradley leaped to his feet and accused Frost Johnson, a Medical College watcher, of passing something surreptitiously to Dr. Tanner. The faster promptly became hysterical and screamed that Johnson had only handed him a sponge.

"Soup!" cried Dr. Bradley. "Full of soup! What do you want with a sponge?"

"I like sponges," said Dr. Tanner, greatly upset.

Repeating his accusation that the sponge had been dripping with soup, Dr. Bradley ordered the watchers of the Neurological Society to leave the hall, and declared that the Society would have nothing further to do with the experiment. A few hours later both Johnson and Dr. Tanner formally denied, in writing, that the sponge had contained food, and said that Dr. Tanner had used it to wipe his face. This explanation was considered at a special meeting of the Society, which finally decided to send its watchers back to their posts and continue its observations. The Medical College and independent watchers agreed not to hand anything to Dr. Tanner until it had been inspected by Dr. Bradley or his associates.

On the first day of his fast Dr. Tanner drank two ounces of water, but thereafter drank no more until the eleventh day, when he swallowed four ounces, after having walked nine laps around his enclosure. On July 14, the sixteenth day of the experiment, he went riding in a barouche with Drs. Gunn and Bradley. They stopped at the Brunswick Hotel, where Dr. Tanner drank two ounces of water, and again at a spring in Central Park near East One Hundred and Third Street, where he drank ten ounces from a gourd. After he swallowed the draught, Dr. Tanner exclaimed:

"Ah! What wonderful water!"

This innocent remark was destined to have extraordinary consequences. The newspapers duly chronicled the fact that Dr. Tanner had been greatly impressed by the water of the Central Park spring, and that he had ordered a gallon demijohn to be filled with it and taken to Clarendon Hall for future use. Almost immediately rumors began to circulate that Dr. Tanner's success as a faster was due entirely to the use of the spring water, and he was quoted throughout the city as having said that if drunk freely, this water would cure any disease known to medical science. He never said anything of the sort, of course, but a widespread belief that the water of the Central Park spring possessed remarkable curative properties persisted in New York for more than thirty years; as late at 1912 people were still carrying away the water in bottles, or rubbing it on their rheumatic limbs. The idea that the water was a cure-all was not abandoned until the Park Commission had it analyzed, and reported that it contained nothing not found in other water.

Thirty days after the beginning of the fast Dr. Tanner had lost more than twenty-five pounds, and several of the watching physicians began to worry about his health. They declared that he had already fasted longer than any other mortal, and urged him to quit, which he promised to do if he began to hiccup. However, he didn't hiccup, and so continued to do without food for the full forty days. Doctors from all over the world wrote long letters telling him how to break his fast without harm to his stomach. One advised him to take five drops of milk and nothing more for twenty-four hours, and another suggested that he smell a plate of buttered toast for half an hour before attempting to eat anything.

None of this advice was followed. Dr. Tanner had his own ideas about the resumption of normal gastronomic exercises, and they were carried out, to the huge delight of the great crowd which assembled to watch him start eating again. During the morning of the last day, August 7, a long table was carried into the hall and piled high with delicacies, including half a dozen bottles of Russian milk wine and six huge Georgia watermelons. At eleven o'clock Dr. Tanner stepped on the scales, and Drs. Gunn and Bradley announced that he weighed 121½, having lost thirty-six pounds. His general health, they reported, was good. At half past eleven a small boy, dressed in his Sunday best, entered the enclosure, made a little speech, and handed Dr. Tanner a peach. The faster sat in his rocking-chair and began to pare

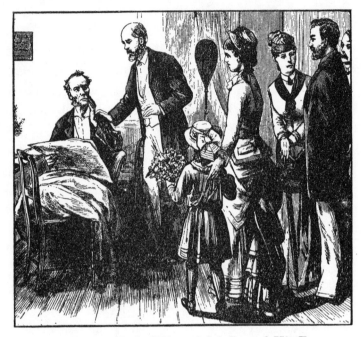

Dr. Tanner on the Thirty-eighth Day of His Fast

the fruit, meanwhile singing a hymn in a low voice. At twelve
o'clock sharp Dr. Gunn blew his whistle, whereupon Dr. Tanner
held his peach aloft for a moment and then ate it with obvious
relish. As he spat out the seed, the crowd cheered madly.

The peach having been disposed of Dr. Gunn and Dr. Bradley
escorted Dr. Tanner to the table, where the hero carefully
smelled each item of food. He then drank half a glass of milk,
and at ten minutes past twelve left the hall and went with Dr.
Gunn to the latter's home, in West Twenty-fourth Street. At
three o'clock in the afternoon he ate a pound of watermelon and
a half-pound of beefsteak, and during the next twenty-four
hours he ate heartily every two hours, when he was not sleeping.
Within three days he had regained ten of his thirty-six lost
pounds and had returned to his normal diet.

For two or three weeks Dr. Tanner was exhibited at Huber's Museum in Fourteenth Street, admission fifty cents, but New York soon forgot him. He didn't appear in the news again, so far as the metropolis was concerned, until 1901, when he suggested that poor people should train themselves to hibernate during the cold weather. On his eightieth birthday, in 1911, he announced that when he was a hundred he would fast eighty days and then marry, but he didn't live long enough to perform either of these feats. He died on December 29, 1918, in the County Hospital at San Diego, California.

Dr. Tanner's forty-day fast remained the American record until 1888, when John Zachar, of Racine, Wisconsin, fasted fifty-three days under supervision. The Tanner mark was again bettered in 1890, when Giovanni Succi, an Italian seaman, went without food for forty-five days at the Koster & Bial Music Hall in West Twenty-third Street.

THE GREAT ROCKING-CHAIR SCANDAL

COMPARATIVELY FEW New Yorkers visited Central Park on Saturday, June 22, 1901, because the weather was cool and balmy, and greater attractions were to be found elsewhere. Those who did, however, were pleasantly surprised to find, near the Casino and along the Mall, rows of bright green rocking-chairs, instead of the hard benches upon which they had been accustomed to sit. About half of the new seats were armchairs. Blessing Tammany Hall and the city fathers, a hundred or more citizens promptly ensconced themselves in the comfortable, cane-bottomed rockers. Just as promptly two men, smartly uniformed in gray and carrying black satchels slung over their shoulders, appeared and demanded five cents from the occupant of each arm-chair, and three cents from each of those who had chosen a less pretentious seat. There was considerable grumbling, but the majority paid. Those who refused to do so were summarily ejected. To every question the collectors had the same reply:

"Them's Mr. Spate's chairs."

The newspapers were still very busy with the Philippine insurrection, which had ended only three months before with the capture of Aguinaldo by General Funston, but space was found next morning for brief items about the extraordinary new feature of Central Park. That afternoon reporters called upon George C. Clausen, president of the Park Commission, and asked why it was now necessary to pay for seats in a public park. Mr. Clausen talked freely. It appeared that a man calling himself Oscar F. Spate, whom Mr. Clausen had never seen before, had walked casually into the offices of the Park Commission and said that he would like to place a few chairs in the parks and charge people for sitting in them. He explained that this was the custom in Paris and London, and that it would doubtless be a very good thing for New York, to say nothing of Mr. Spate. Without troubling the other members of the Commission with such a trivial matter, Mr. Clausen gave Mr. Spate a five-year contract, under which Mr. Spate agreed to pay the city $500 a year for the privilege of installing chairs in the parks of Manhattan and Staten Island. Mr. Spate then ordered 6,000 chairs, at a cost of about $1.50 each, which he estimated would give him a potential gross revenue of between $250 and $300 a day. Later a man (name not mentioned), who said he spoke for Mr. Spate, announced that the rockingchair magnate had already put $30,000 into the scheme. The reporters figured that the chairs and the contract had cost about $9,500, and innocently asked how the remaining $20,500 had been expended.

"Well," said the spokesman, vaguely, "there's always expenses in a thing like this, you know."

Mr. Spate himself was finally found in a little cubby-hole of an office in the St. James Building. He gave this statement to the newspapers:

"I'll put in as many chairs as the Park Board will allow. The attendants who collect the charges are in my pay. They will wear gray uniforms, and each will look after about fifty chairs, from 10 A.M. to 10 P.M. A five-cent ticket entitles the holder to sit in either a five-cent or a three-cent chair in any park at any time during that one day, but the holder of a three-cent ticket can sit only in a three-cent chair."

Further, Mr. Spate warmly defended his plan on the ground that the charge for the rockers would serve to keep the dirty loungers out of the parks. This statement aroused much indignation. Various city officials immediately announced that above all things they were friends of the poor, and President Guggenheim of the Municipal Council added that he "saw no good reason for allowing private parties to occupy park ground and make money through a scheme like this." The Central Federated Union adopted a satirical resolution urging the city to barricade the parks and admit only the clean and prosperous, and sent it to the Park Commission, together with a serious resolution vigorously denouncing both Mr. Clausen and Mr. Spate. The *Tribune* said editorially that it was "only another instance of the hopeless stupidity of the present Park Commission," but the *Times* favored the idea, provided prices were properly regulated. The *Journal*, of course, flew at once to the colors in violent defense of the right of the poor man to sit in the public parks. Commissioner Clausen pointed out that there were always plenty of free benches except on Saturdays and Sundays and holidays, and the *Tribune* said caustically that those were the only days on which there was any great demand for seats. A resolution demanding an investigation was introduced by a Republican member of the Board of Aldermen, but was immediately killed.

Meanwhile Mr. Spate had put more chairs in Central Park, and long rows of the green rockers also appeared in Madison Square. Those who tried to use them without paying were thrown out by Spate's collectors, many of whom were unnecessarily rough. Despite the increasing discontent, however, there was no actual trouble for several days. If Nature hadn't come to the rescue of the poor man, it is likely that within a few weeks the excitement would have died a natural death. The chairs would have remained, and their numbers would have been increased. In a year or so New York would have acquired the habit of paying for seats in the public parks, and would probably still be doing so to this day.

On Wednesday, June 26, 1901, the thermometer at the Weather Bureau registered ninety degrees above zero at 11:45 A.M., and again at 4:00 P.M. This marked the beginning of one of the hottest periods New York has ever experienced. The next day, Thursday, the temperature was again ninety degrees, and three deaths were reported. On Friday, June 28, the thermometer registered ninety-four degrees, and on Saturday a maximum temperature of ninety-two degrees caused sixteen deaths. Fifteen more persons died on Sunday, which, with a temperature of ninety-seven degrees, was the hottest June day since the establishment of the Weather Bureau in 1871. Monday was somewhat cooler, but on Tuesday, July 2, the thermometer registered ninety-nine degrees in the shade. It was the hottest day New York had experienced in twenty years. Two hundred deaths were reported, the ambulance-drivers of the various hospitals were so busy that they went without sleep for twenty-four hours, and the city ordered the parks kept open all night. Wednesday, July 3, was five degrees cooler, but there were 317 deaths, and fifty-seven on July 4, when the temperature dropped to eighty-six degrees. For the next four or five days the thermometer remained around ninety degrees, but the humidity was lower, and there were fewer fatalities. From June 28 to July 4, inclusive, there were 382 deaths and 521 prostrations in Manhattan alone, and 797 deaths and 891 prostrations in the metropolitan district.

It was this wave of torrid heat that brought disaster to Mr. Spate's ambitious plans. New York flocked almost *en masse* to the parks, only to find that the Park Commission had suddenly decided to remove a great many of the free benches for repairs. Most of those which remained had been moved into the broiling sunshine and were actually too hot to sit upon. Mr. Spate's handsome rockers, however, were under the shade trees and the bushes, in the only places where even the slightest degree of comfort might be found.

The first rioting occurred in Madison Square on the afternoon of July 6, when a man sat in a rocking-chair and refused to pay five cents, suggesting that Mr. Spate's collector, Thomas Tulley, go to hell and take Mr. Spate with him. Tulley promptly pulled the chair from under him, and a crowd which had been standing around jeering Tulley began to shout: "Lynch him! He's Spate's man!" With the angry mob at his heels Tulley fled across the street into the Fifth Avenue Hotel, where he was rushed upstairs and locked in a bedroom. The crowd milled about the hotel lobby for half an hour or so and then returned to the park, while Tulley was escorted home by policemen. Later in the afternoon the Madison Square crowd attacked another Spate hireling who had ejected a boy from one of the rocking-chairs. A policeman who tried to interfere was thrown into the park fountain. Mr. Spate's collectors fled, and throughout the remainder of the day members of the mob took turns sitting in the comfortable rockers. Several were carried away as souvenirs.

On Sunday, July 7, a crowd of young men and boys annoyed Spate's collectors near the Casino in Central Park by marching back and forth before the rows of chairs. As they marched they sang loudly, to the tune of "Sweet Annie Moore," a popular ballad of the period:

> We pay no more,
> We pay no more;
> No more we pay for park
> Chairs any more.
> Clausen made a break,
> One summer's day;
> And now he ain't
> Commishner no more.

A large crowd quickly gathered, and became so threatening that Mr. Spate's few paying customers abandoned the chairs they had rented and hurriedly left the park. Thereupon the mob swarmed into the rows of rockers, smashing a dozen and carrying away as many more. One of Mr. Spate's attendants quit his job and went home, but another made a half-hearted attempt to collect his fees. He quit also, however, when a woman jabbed him from behind with a hatpin.

The next day, July 8, there was trouble in Madison Square. A score of boys went from chair to chair, sitting as long as they pleased. They were accompanied and supported by a crowd which repeatedly threatened to lynch the attendants if they interfered. One of Mr. Spate's men, Otto Beerman, slapped a boy, and was immediately escorted out of the park by half a dozen policemen, who had great difficulty protecting him. Throughout the day there was almost continuous rioting in Madison Square, although the reserves from the West Thirtieth Street police station succeeded in preventing the destruction of more than a dozen chairs. About the mid-

Cartoon by F. Opper from the New York Journal, *July 8, 1901 (by courtesy of the* New York Journal*)*

dle of the afternoon two young men took possession of two of the rockers and loudly offered a reward of a thousand dollars to any of Mr. Spate's attendants who would throw them out. Two tried and were promptly knocked down, whereupon the crowd cheered wildly, and enthusiastically kicked and pummeled their fallen foes. One of the young men hurled two of the rockers into the basin of the park fountain, and announced that thereafter he would destroy a rocker every time he struck a Spate collector. He was not again disturbed, for by this time he had been recognized as Terry McGovern, featherweight champion of the world. His companion was Joe Humphreys, now the well-known prize-fight announcer. Six other chair-sitters, however, were arrested by the police and marched to the West Thirtieth Street station. Each was followed by more than two hundred men and boys, marching in lock-step and chanting:

> Spate! Spate!
> Clausen and Spate!
> Spate! Spate!
> Clausen and Spate!

Rioting continued in both Madison Square and Central Park during the next few days, an enormous mob invading Madison Square on the evening of July 9, smashing many of Mr. Spate's chairs and driving the collectors away. Police Commissioner Michael Murphy forbade the police to help Mr. Spate's men collect money for the use of the chairs, and later ordered the cops to make no arrests except on warrants properly sworn out before magistrates, several of whom announced that they would think twice before issuing warrants for disorder in the parks. Commissioner Clausen told the newspapers that he regretted the turn that events had taken, but that only the Park Board could revoke Mr. Spate's contract, although the Commission had nothing to do with making it. A few hours later he reversed this opinion and said that he would immediately cancel the contract, whereupon Mr. Spate obtained a court injunction restraining Mr. Clausen and the Park Commission from interfering with him. Later this writ was dismissed. Mr. Clausen then asked the Board of Estimate to provide five thousand new park benches, and with much oratory in behalf of the poor man the Board appropriated twenty thousand dollars. And no more was ever heard of that.

The situation had now become so serious that in both Central Park and Madison Square Mr. Spate piled his chairs in heaps and rented them only when paid in advance. As soon as a customer rented a chair, however, the crowd smashed it, or passed it along from hand to hand until it vanished, later to ornament someone's flat. Throngs of men and boys also made raids upon the piles of chairs, and when they were not doing this they kept up a constant bombardment with stones against Spate's attendants. Several times Mr. Spate himself appeared in the parks, but invariably left in a hurry, escorted by a yelling crowd.

On July 11 Max Radt, vice-president of the Jefferson State Bank, obtained a Supreme Court injunction restraining Spate and the Park Commission from charging for park seats. The writ was served upon Spate early the next morning, and he promptly put all of his chairs in storage, except two in Madison Square, which he had rented. The occupants refused to accept their money back. They said they had engaged the chairs in good faith and intended to sit in them all day. They did, too. The crowd kept them supplied with food and water, and when they occasionally got up to stretch their legs, delegations accompanied them, carrying the chairs and fighting off Spate's attendants. When the customers finally left they took the chairs with them.

Several other citizens obtained injunctions against Spate within the next few days, and he at length announced that he would abandon his project. He dropped out of sight as quickly as he had appeared. The *Tribune* asked editorially: "Who is Oscar F. Spate?" but the question was never answered.

A week or two later, on July 29, the Park Commission announced that Mr. Clausen personally had purchased all of the Spate chairs and had presented them to the city to be placed in the parks and lettered plainly: "For the Exclusive Use of Women and Children." Moreover, Mr. Clausen had requested that the word "FREE" be painted on them in large letters.

CHAPTER 4

THE BROOKLYN ENIGMA

IN THE summer of 1850, a few months before the New York Central Railroad ran its first train from New York to Albany, James E. and Elizabeth Crosby Fancher moved to Brooklyn from Attleboro, Massachusetts, where they had conducted a small retail store, and built a modest home at No. 160 Gates Avenue. With them came their two-year-old daughter, Mary J., called Mollie, a frail child who caused her mother much concern. According to her statements in later years, Mrs. Fancher frequently had premonitions that Mollie was destined for a life of pain and trouble. When she was dying, in 1860, she called her sister, Miss Susan E. Crosby, to her bedside, and said:

"Mollie, I can see, is a child of sorrow, and will need your care. I want you to make me one promise: that if anything happens to her you will look after her and care for her as for your own daughter."

Miss Crosby promised, and tried to make light of Mrs. Fancher's dire forebodings. But they were more than fulfilled. In 1864 Mollie Fancher was thrown from a horse while riding in Prospect Park, and her head struck against the pavement. Thereafter she was subject to fainting spells and violent headaches. A year later, on June 8, 1865, she was dragged a block by a Fulton Street trolley car, which she had attempted to leave while it was still in motion. Her spine was injured, and her nervous system completely deranged. She was able to be about, though ill, until February 3, 1866. On the morning of that day, while helping Miss Crosby can preserves, she suddenly shrieked, stood on her toes, and spun around like a top. Then she bent forward, clasped her feet in both hands, and began rolling about the kitchen floor like a hoop. She was carried to her bed, and didn't leave it for fifty years and eight days, until she died, on February 11, 1916.

During much of that time she was blind, paralyzed, and helpless. Her sufferings were constant and intense, despite the efforts of many physicians, among them such eminent practitioners as Dr. Samuel Fleet Speir, Dr. Robert Speir, Dr. Robert Ormiston, and Dr. Willard Parker, for whom the present Willard Parker Hospital was named. Their diagnoses agreed that the principal cause of her illness was the terrific shock to her nervous system, and that there was also considerable mental disturbance. They tried every treatment that the greatest medical minds of the age could conceive; among other things, they changed the position of her bed so that she lay in line with the magnetic currents of the earth, and placed a large horseshoe magnet at her feet. Even that, however, failed to provide relief.

Miss Fancher's illness presented interesting problems to the medical profession, but other aspects of her case brought her international renown. She was not only New York's most celebrated invalid; she was also the psychological marvel of her time. For more than thirty years, until she lost her supposedly supernatural powers, her clairvoyant gifts and her uncanny exploits in the realms of second sight astounded a continuous procession of doctors, scientists, professors, and ministers of the gospel. So great was her fame that P. T. Barnum repeatedly tried, without success, to induce her to make an exhibition tour under his management, offering to provide for her comfort a mattress stuffed with swansdown and a bed plated with gold. The sightseer from the hinterland considered his trip to the metropolis a failure unless it included a visit to Miss Fancher's little store on the ground floor of the house in Gates Avenue, where embroidery, crocheting, and wax flowers in intricate and handsome designs, all fashioned by the skilled hands of the noted invalid, were offered for sale. If Miss Fancher's condition permitted, an occasional pilgrim who bore the proper credentials was admitted to her apartment above the store, where she lived with three parrots, six canaries, three cats, four huge bowls of goldfish, and her aunt, Miss Crosby.

Miss Fancher's psychical powers were carefully investigated by each of her physicians; by reporters from the *Sun*, the *Herald*, the *Times*, the Brooklyn *Daily Eagle*, and innumerable other newspapers, who wrote scores of articles meticulously describing her miraculous feats; and by at least a dozen prominent citizens of Brooklyn and Manhattan, among them Henry M. Parkhurst, a noted astronomer; Will Carleton, the poet;

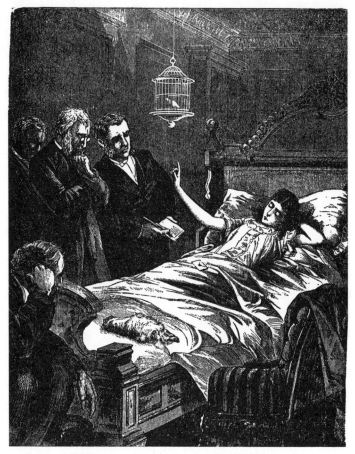

Mollie Fancher Astounds the Scientists
(This picture, from a magazine of the period, shows her left arm
immovable behind her head. In reality it was her right arm
that was so effected.)

Epes Sargent, a well-known author and playwright; Professor
Charles E. West, principal of the Brooklyn Heights Seminary;
and Judge Abram H. Dailey, who made a report on the
Fancher case before the Psychical Congress at the first
Chicago World's Fair. In later years Judge Dailey wrote a book

about Miss Fancher called *The Brooklyn Enigma,* a heavy tome filled with affidavits and detailed statements by the many investigators. Each of the latter declared that to his absolute knowledge Miss Fancher was able to perform these wonders:

She could distinguish colors in the darkness, and also during the years in which she was blind.

She could find mislaid articles.

She could describe the dress and doings of friends and relatives fifty miles away.

She could tell the time of day by passing her hand across a watch-crystal, and across the room without looking at the clock.

She knew when a thunderstorm was approaching several hours before it appeared.

She knew that the fire-bells were going to ring five minutes before they did so.

She could read letters and books by running her hands over them, or by putting them, unopened, beneath the bed-clothes. Dr. Samuel Fleet Speir said that on one occasion he received from the postman a letter addressed to Miss Crosby, and took it into the house with him. While he held the letter, still sealed, in his hand, Miss Fancher wrote it exactly, word for word, on a slate. As a further test Dr. Speir asked her to write the contents of another letter, addressed to himself and delivered to his office, which he had not opened and of which she could not possibly have had previous knowledge. She did so without a mistake. A similar experiment was made by Dr. Parkhurst, the astronomer, with part of a page cut from a book chosen at random in his library in the darkness, and which he had not read. He placed it in a thick envelope, and Miss Fancher wrote for him the name of the book, the number of the page, and, except for one figure, everything that was on it, even parts of words. Dr. Parkhurst described the test in the *Herald* of November 30, 1878.

Miss Fancher's mysterious powers also enabled her to identify persons who rang her doorbell before the visitor entered the house. Perhaps her best-known feat of this sort was performed during the twelfth year of her illness. The bell clanged one afternoon while Miss Fancher was chatting with several friends, and she said to Miss Crosby:

"Aunt, Uncle Ike is at the door, and he is very ill."

She was correct. The caller was her Uncle Ike Crosby, her mother's brother, who had come home from California to die of tuberculosis. Moreover, Uncle Ike had left Brooklyn some twenty-five years before, when Mollie Fancher was about seven years old, and no member of his family had seen or heard of him until he suddenly appeared at the Gates Avenue house.

All of the investigators, particularly the clergymen, were convinced that Miss Fancher frequently held converse with spirits, and Professor West went even further than that. He expressed the opinion that Miss Fancher had often been to heaven. In his report on the case he said:

"I cannot tell you that strangely interesting part of her experience. After she is dead it will be known; but it is more of a revelation than that seen by John from the Isle of Patmos."

Unfortunately, Professor West's death preceded that of Miss Fancher, and apparently she told no one else the details of her celestial travels. In any event, the revelation was not forthcoming when she died.

For more than half of her long illness Miss Fancher was subject to trances, some of which lasted only a few hours, while others continued for days and even weeks and months. The longest was nine years. On the morning of June 3, 1866 Dr. Robert Speir called to see her and remained an hour. When he started to leave, he looked at his watch and remarked that he would be late for dinner.

"We're having chicken pot pie today," he said, "and you know that's never good when cold."

That afternoon Miss Fancher went into the long trance. Throughout the nine years her eyes remained closed, and for six years her body was cold and rigid, there was no evidence of respiration, her physicians could detect only a slight pulse, and she never spoke. Occasionally she was fed by force, but for months at a time she was given no nourishment except a little water. Later Dr. Samuel Speir, in one of his reports, said that during the first thirteen years of her illness, during which he called upon her at least once each day, she had received less food than a normal woman of her age and size would consume in forty-eight hours. He also described various tests which he had made to prove that she had not eaten while he was away.

During the last three years of the long trance Miss Fancher's body relaxed to some extent, she spoke once in a while, and she was able to move her left arm with considerable freedom. In that time she wrote 6,500 letters, a score of poems and lyric prayers, worked up a hundred thousand ounces of worsted yarn into crocheted patterns, made a satin waist and a pleated lining for her coffin, did a great deal of fine embroidery, and fashioned many designs in wax flowers. All of this labor was performed with her eyes closed and her right arm held rigidly behind her head. According to Miss Crosby, she had never before embroidered or worked in wax.

When Miss Fancher awoke to full consciousness, her life

was apparently resumed exactly where it had been interrupted nine years before. Dr. Robert Speir's brother, Dr. Samuel Fleet Speir, was at her bedside, and she said to him:

"Well, doctor, did your brother get home in time for his chicken pot pie?"

In the summer of 1878, about three years after the end of the nine-year trance, there began another curious phase of Miss Fancher's illness, which was also characterized by psychical manifestations. This was the development of five distinct identities, or personalities, which took possession of the invalid's consciousness at different times while she was in the shorter trances, with appropriate changes in facial expression, in manner of speaking, and in topics of conversation. They were called Idol, Sunbeam, Ruby, Pearl, and Rosebud, names which were bestowed upon them by Miss Fancher's friend George F. Sargent, with whom she was associated in the manufacture of various appliances for the use of cripples. The first to appear was Idol, and the others were first noticed at intervals during the succeeding six months. All were present, though it would be too much to say that they were properly accounted for, by the first of January 1879.

Sunbeam was the nearest to Miss Fancher's ordinary personality, and was the most powerful of the ghostly identities; sometimes she drove the others away, announcing her presence with the brisk statement that there was work to be done. She was the only one who, on her first appearance, seemed to recognize Miss Crosby and several friends of Miss Fancher who were in the room. The others had to be introduced and were always shy in the presence of strangers. They appeared regularly several times a week, but, with the exception of Sunbeam, always at night. Sunbeam preferred the jolly daylight hours and was in the ascendancy as long as the sun shone. She managed the affairs of the house as well as Miss Fancher did in her normal personality, and also did the fine embroidery, crocheting, and wax-flower designs. When Miss Fancher was Idol, she professed to have no recollection of the trolley accident. Idol was very jealous of Sunbeam and always tried to hide or destroy the work which the latter had accomplished. Moreover, Idol was inclined to be morose; she often wept bitterly, complaining that she had no friends and that no one loved her.

Rosebud was a child of some six or seven years. When Miss Fancher was under the influence of this personality, she wrote long communications to "Papa and Mamma," laboriously printing each letter. She was also a great talker, prattling incessantly in baby lingo. But she made up for this, to some extent, by being a gifted mimic; she could imitate the cackling of hens, the mewing of cats, the bleating of sheep, the grunting of pigs, and the neighing of horses.

Pearl was a very spiritual young lady, cultured, modest, and agreeable, whose conversation dealt principally with poetry and the finer things of life. She possessed a clear recollection of events in Miss Fancher's life prior to the sixteenth year, when she was injured. It was when Miss Fancher was Pearl that she wrote her many poems, including a lyric prayer which received wide circulation.

Ruby was also a young lady, but was the direct antithesis of Pearl. She was dashing and vivacious, even hoydenish, and very gifted in repartee. As George F. Sargent put it in an exhaustive report on the five personalities into which Miss Fancher was so frequently transformed, "Ruby comes with a bound and a shout and leaves the same way."

The newspaper articles about Mollie Fancher's psychical powers, and the published reports of her friends, were not,

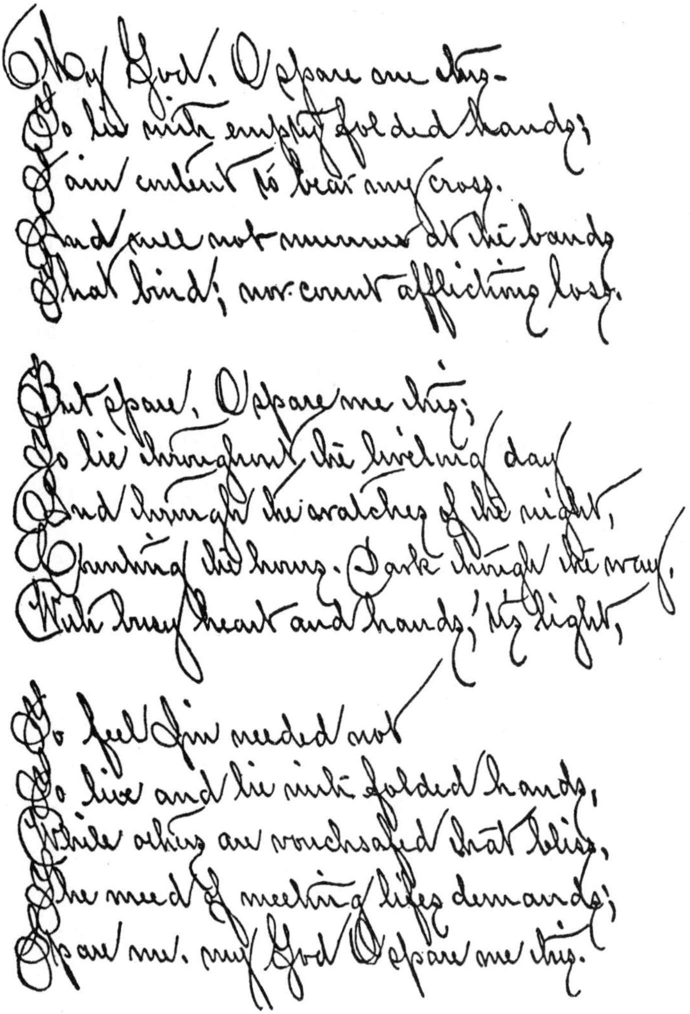

Oh My God, O spare me this—
To lie with empty folded hands;
I am content to bear my cross.
And will not murmur at the bands
That bind; nor count afflicting loss.

But spare, O spare me this;
To lie throughout the livelong day
And through the watches of the night,
Counting the hours. Dark though the way,
With busy heart and hands, 'tis light,

To feel I'm needed not
To live and lie with folded hands,
While others are vouchsafed that bliss,
The need of meeting life's demands;
Spare me, my God O spare me this.

Mollie Fancher's Prayer, in Her Own Handwriting

of course, accepted without question by everyone who heard or read of the case. There were many physicians and laymen and even a few clergymen who denounced her as a fraud and an impostor. Perhaps her severest critics were two of New York's most distinguished physicians, Dr. George M. Beard and Dr. William A. Hammond, the latter of whom had been Surgeon-General of the United States Army. In an article published in the *Sun* on November 23, 1878, Dr. Beard declared that he had received proof that "Mollie Fancher intentionally deceives, that she lives on the fat of the land, that the fancy articles she professes to make are made for her, that her reading without eyes is done by trickery." However, he refused to produce the proof. Three days later Dr. Hammond said in an interview with a *Sun* reporter that Mollie Fancher was a faker and a liar, and that she was a typical case of simulative hysteria. The value of these opinions was greatly lessened by the fact that neither Dr. Hammond nor Dr. Beard had ever seen or examined Miss Fancher, and both refused to do so, although she invited them to visit her and make whatever inquiry they pleased. It remained a matter of record that everyone who did investigate the case was convinced that Miss Fancher possessed mysterious gifts not bestowed upon ordinary mortals.

In 1894 the Section on Psychology of the New York Medico-Legal Society proposed a scientific inquiry into Miss Fancher's occult doings, but she refused to receive the investigators, on the advice of Judge Abram H. Dailey. The latter explained, in the newspapers and later in his book, that the Society's action came too late to be fair to Miss Fancher. By that time her physical condition had shown marked improvement; she was no longer totally blind; she could use both arms, and her body above the waist; she was able to absorb nourishment and had gained greatly in weight and strength. This improvement had been accompanied by a gradual withdrawal of psychic powers, which continued as her general health improved. By the middle eighteen-nineties they had vanished entirely, whereupon the newspapers and the public promptly forgot her and hurried on to the next sensation. Thereafter Miss Fancher was nothing more than a bedridden old woman with a passion for fancy embroidery and crocheting.

On February 3, 1916 she invited her friends, and also President Wilson, who couldn't come, to attend a "Golden Jubilee Testimonial at her home." Eight days later she died.

CHAPTER 5

THE QUEEN OF HACKENSACK

DURING THE late summer of 1863—the year of Lincoln's Emancipation Proclamation and the Battle of Gettysburg—the inhabitants of Hackensack, New Jersey, then a fashionable suburb, were greatly interested in a huge, many-roomed mansion which was being erected on the outskirts of the village. There was much mystery about the house, for the builder refused to divulge any information about his client, save that she was a rich widow called Madame Adelaide Kleinschmidt. The workmen, who had been imported from New York, knew nothing except that they received the unusually high wage of a dollar and a quarter a day.

Presently great cases and boxes of furniture arrived from

New York's most exclusive stores, and six servants, clad in resplendent livery, went with great aloofness about the task of making the mansion habitable. Tradesmen reported that the interior was of a surpassing elegance. Thick rugs and carpets covered the floors; lounges, ottomans, sofas, and easy-chairs, stuffed with horsehair of the finest quality and richly upholstered in brilliantly brocaded silks and satins, were scattered in lavish profusion about the rooms; handsome paintings adorned the walls; and voluptuous statuary crowded

The Queen of Hackensack

the halls and vestibules. Nor were the grounds less charming. In the gardens, fountains of various shapes whirled fragrant spray high into the New Jersey sky, and the lawn was dotted with cast-iron deer and other stylish animals. The hitching post, at the end of a long graveled driveway which wound gracefully between formal rows of flower-bushes, was a gigantic iron elk, with a tremendous spread of antlers.

Early in September the village florist was instructed to deliver a large bouquet of his choicest blooms daily at the mansion, and the veterinarian as notified to hold himself in readiness for frequent attendance upon Madame Kleinschmidt's valuable lap-dogs, of which she possessed a half-dozen.

A few days later a magnificent coach, with bright red wheels, a glossy green body, and yellow satin lining and upholstery, rolled grandly down the graveled driveway, and thence over the cobblestones into the village. It was drawn by four milk-white horses accoutered in gold-mounted harnesses, and on the box sat a coachman liveried in blue and silver, cracking a long black whip with a curling crimson lash. Behind were two footmen similarly attired, one of whom, from time to time, blew loudly upon a silver trumpet. Amidst the satin cushions, in a studied attitude of languorous condescension, reclined Madame Kleinschmidt, a sensuous brunette of some thirty years. Diamonds sparkled at her throat and upon her fingers; shining golden bracelets clasped her white wrists, and her svelte figure was provokingly displayed in a gown of rich green velvet, cut in the latest mode and tastily trimmed with satin and fine lace. As her bizarre vehicle rattled and bounced over the uneven pavement, she calmly, even insolently, surveyed the startled villagers through a jeweled quizzing-glass. It is not too much to say that she created a sensation.

Daily thereafter Madame Kleinschmidt took the air, while all Hackensack gaped at her extraordinary equipage and hummed with speculation as to her identity. Many stories were afloat. Some had it that she was the widow of a Cuban sugar king; others that she was the relict of a California millionaire who had found a gold mine after years of toil and privation and had immediately expired of delight; still others that she was the niece of a Southern cotton-planter who had been murdered by his rebellious slaves. The mystery was intensified by the fact that Madame Kleinschmidt invariably spent two days of each week in New York. Not until several weeks had passed, however, did she see fit to dispel the rumors and disclose her secret. Then she confided to the florist, who promptly told everyone else in the village, that she was the granddaughter of an English merchant who had bequeathed her a colossal fortune amassed in the East Indian spice trade. Wearied by the incessant demands of European society, she had come to the United States, and had chosen Hackensack for her home because of its atmosphere of culture and refinement. On her periodical trips to New York, she said, she visited an aged aunt and consulted her banker about her investments.

Having thus revealed herself as a woman of wealth, wisdom, and discernment, Madame Kleinschmidt took a pew in the most fashionable church and launched an attack upon the social citadels of Hackensack. She was victorious almost immediately, for, as we are assured by the celebrated New York detective Phil Farley, who described her career in his book *Criminals of America; or, Tales of the Lives of Thieves, Enabling Every One to Be His Own Detective*, her full-blown, spectacular beauty "soon maddened the male population of the village," and the women flocked to her side to protect and recapture their husbands and sweethearts. They came in anger and annoyance and remained in awe, for Madame Kleinschmidt was highly accomplished in the arts and graces of society. Moreover, she talked very glibly and convincingly about London and Paris and displayed a proper snootiness toward the pretensions of uncouth New Yorkers and Bostonians. Within a few months she was the recognized social arbiter of the village, and she became the uncrowned Queen of Hackensack soon after the Christmas holidays, when she gave a grand ball at her mansion. It was by far the most elaborate function in the history of the town and was attended by the flower and chivalry of the New Jersey countryside.

There was one Hackensack social leader, however, who held aloof and refused to succumb to the overtures and blandishments of the rich widow. Perhaps because of the prominence of her family connections, neither the police records nor the literary works of Detective Farley reveal the name of this rebellious lady; she is referred to simply as Mrs. Blank. She disliked Madame Kleinschmidt at first sight, and did not hesitate to say so. She declined to be introduced, and when asked why she did not call at the mansion or attend the widow's parties, she replied: "What? *I* call upon that unspeakably vulgar creature!" As was not unusual in the New Jersey of the period, Mrs. Blank had a husband, who was described by Detective Farley as "upright, ruggedly honest, yet gentle, deep, and affectionate." He was also "tall, handsome, alert, and wealthy." Moreover, his attitude toward Madame Kleinschmidt did not coincide with that of his spouse. On the contrary, having met her at church, he was dazzled by her splendor and soon became her most ardent admirer. He spent so much time at her home, drinking and carousing in a genteel manner, that Mrs. Blank finally began to understand that his affections were being estranged from her. Her cup of woe was filled almost to overflowing when kind friends began hinting that Mr. Blank was making a fool of himself.

"Stung to the soul by these open insults," wrote Detective Farley, "the poor wife crept closer into herself and only wept the more in secret. One day, in the bitterest hour of all her sufferings, Heaven sent a ray of light, of hope, of comfort— she hugged the happy messenger tightly to her breast and went on dreaming until she thought she saw her husband at her knees in ecstasy, and heard a small voice babbling 'Mother.' Now the wife and woman sprang up within her to the full height of majesty and dignity, and she resolved upon one mighty effort—such as a loving woman alone can make—for her husband's rescue!"[1]

But Mr. Blank was not informed that he was soon to become a father, and so continued upon his mad career of infatuation, blind to the sweet significance of the tiny garments upon which his wife sewed late into the night. Soon, however, the demon of jealousy perched upon his shoulder and whispered into his ear: "What about those trips to New York? Is the widow two-timing you?" Confused and puzzled, Mr. Blank questioned Madame Kleinschmidt, who became indignant at his lack of faith and denied vehemently that she was carrying on an amour in the metropolis. He was not satisfied, however, and he followed her when she next crossed the river on one of the uncertain little boats which were the only ferries that plied the Hudson in those days. And he was himself followed by his wife, who had donned male attire to escape recognition. She succeeded, and not until long afterwards did her husband know that she was the graceful boy who on that day had kept so close at his heels.

Madame Kleinschmidt went directly to a house in Thirty-fourth Street, but after a few moments again appeared. She had changed her dress and now wore a voluminous garment which seemed to be fairly plastered with large pockets. She walked swiftly toward the Broadway shopping district, and from the shelter of an areaway Mrs. Blank saw her husband

---

[1]One gathers from this passage, with apologies to Walter Winchell, that Mrs. Blank anticipated a blessed event.

mount the stoop of an adjoining house and speak to an old woman who answered his knock. He was beaming when he came down the steps, and Mrs. Blank surmised that he had made inquiries about Madame Kleinschmidt and had received pleasant information. She herself inquired after her husband had gone, and was told that, so far as the old lady knew, the house which Madame Kleinschmidt had entered was occupied by a woman whose rich niece lived in New Jersey and often visited her. But Mrs. Blank was not satisfied. She waited, and when Madame Kleinschmidt returned, she was struck by the fact that the widow's pockets fairly bulged with a multitude of unwrapped articles.

Early in the following week Mrs. Blank again came to New York, this time in the proper clothing of her sex. Ostensibly she came to visit her mother, but instead she went to the home of an old school-friend, whose name appears to have been Belle. With their faces hidden by veils, Mrs. Blank and Belle watched the house in Thirty-fourth Street. When Madame Kleinschmidt sallied forth, they followed and kept close behind her as she walked up and down Broadway and mingled with the crowd of shoppers. Suddenly Belle clutched Mrs. Blank's arm and exclaimed:

"Look, Kate! Look!"

"God in heaven!" cried Mrs. Blank. "She's a thief!"

For the Queen of Hackensack had picked a lady's pocket!

"What shall we do?" asked Belle. "We must trap her!"

"We shall see the police," said Mrs. Blank.

A few days later, when Madame Kleinschmidt sent out invitations to a dance, Mrs. Blank announced that she would attend, and urged her friends to be present also. To their exclamations of surprise she returned only a cryptic smile.

Came, then, the night of the ball.

"The spacious and lavishly embellished halls of the Klein-schmidt mansion were brilliantly lighted," wrote Detective Farley, "and many guests moved to and fro. Music, laughter, and fragrance filled the air. Never was the mistress of the *fête* more gorgeously arrayed or in finer feather. Men who thought her good-looking before swore she was beautiful now, and all the women were dying of envy. The supremely happy host-ess flitted about from room to room and guest to guest, all smiles and pretty sayings, when suddenly the Blanks were announced. Her face at that moment was a picture. All the bottled longings of the previous months now burst forth upon her countenance in one overpowering glow of triumph. She moved forward with a majesty of mien almost too stately and grand for earthly conception."

Mrs. Blank's appearance created a profound sensation. Not only was she in ordinary walking costume, but she was accom-panied by a stranger, a stern-faced man with a derby hat and a handsome, flowing mustache. For a moment she stood in the open frame of the doorway "like a lovely picture of virtue rebuking vice." Then she pointed to Madame Kleinschmidt and cried in ringing tones:

"Ladies and gentlemen! This woman is a thief!"

"A thief!" exclaimed a hundred voices.

"It's a lie!" shrieked Madame Kleinschmidt.

"It is God's truth!" said Mrs. Blank, scornfully. "You are even now wearing my emerald ring upon your finger! Do not all of you recognize it? It is the one I received as a prize for selling the most tickets to our bazaar."

Quickly, almost convulsively, Madame Kleinschmidt plunged her hand into the folds of her dress. She was too late. A murmur of horrified recognition arose.

"I trapped you," said Mrs. Blank triumphantly. "You

picked my pocket on Broadway the other day." She beckoned to the stranger. "This man saw you do it. He is a detective!"

"Yes," said the stranger, stepping forward briskly and twirling his mustache, "I am a detective." He tapped

The Queen of Hackensack Dethroned

Madame Kleinschmidt on the shoulder. "The game's up!" he said sternly.

"Well," said Madame Kleinschmidt, laughing shrilly, "I've had a jolly good time and showed up these stupid asses. Are you going back to New York tonight?"

"We are."

After the detective, who was none other than Phil Farley himself, had departed with Madame Kleinschmidt, the victorious wife and prospective mother weepingly embraced her repentant husband, now happily cured of his infatuation. Then she told the abashed social butterflies of Hackensack the bitter truth about their erstwhile Queen, as she had learned it from the New York police.

Madame Kleinschmidt's first name was not even Adelaide. It was Lena, but she was better known to the police throughout the United States and Canada as Black Lena, alias Lizzie Johnson, alias Rice, alias Smith. She was one of the most notorious blackmailers, pickpockets, shop-lifters, and confidence women in the United States, the peer and associate of all the noted female crooks of the day. Her visits to the metropolis had not been for the purpose of visiting an aged aunt; the old woman who had posed as such in the Thirty-fourth Street house was in reality an accomplice, believed by the police to have been Old Mother Hubbard, another well-known underworld character. As a matter of fact, Madame Kleinschmidt had queened it in Hackensack for five days a week and had picked pockets and robbed department stores in New York the other two. She disposed of her loot to Mrs. Fredericka Mandelbaum, better known as Marm, one of the most celebrated fences, or receivers of stolen goods, in the annals of the metropolis. Marm owned a three-story building at Clinton and Rivington Streets. As a blind she operated a haberdashery on the ground floor, but her real business was carried on in a clapboarded wing that sprawled its ungainly length down Rivington Street.

Marm Mandelbaum had always regarded Black Lena Kleinschmidt as one of her cleverest crooks, but she was not clever enough for the outraged wife from Hackensack. After consulting with the police, following her discovery that Madame Kleinschmidt was a thief, Mrs. Blank had trapped the widow by displaying a well-filled purse, containing the emerald ring, in crowded Broadway and then carelessly putting it in her skirt pocket. Black Lena had promptly taken it, but had been observed by the eagle-eyed Detective Farley.

CHAPTER 6

A LADY OF FASHION

NEW YORK society was very gaudy and glittering during the ten years which followed the Civil War, and the fashionable lady of the less conservative element was an even more abject slave to the beauty parlor and to the cosmetic shop than is her modern counterpart. Moreover, her final appearance depended to a great extent upon the skill of the carpenter, the blacksmith, and the steelworker, for Nature's distressing omissions were freely corrected by mechanical artifice. Once arrayed for a *fête*, especially if she had lost the bloom of youth, the butterfly of the eighteen-sixties and the early eighteen-seventies staggered forth under the burden of an infinite variety of beautifying apparatus constructed of steel, iron, wire, cotton, wood, horsehair, and wool, all attached to her person by straps, tape, and mucilage.

Plumpness was the main desideratum of the period, and the stylish female shape was a modification of the hour-glass figure, with a small waist, a tight-fitting bodice cut extremely low, and a very full, billowing skirt. The expansive bosom which such a figure demanded was obtained by a great variety of means, among them the use of a deceptive rubber device called a "patent heaver," which was manufactured in large quantities by a flourishing concern in the Bowery. The dentist was called upon to provide plump cheeks, which he did by filling them out with hard composition pads running upward along each side of the mouth. These were called "plumpers," and some were so large as to give the appearance of mumps. Their greatest drawback, aside from the discomfort, to which, of course, the determined ladies gave no heed, was that they often shifted position, so that a woman wearing them was apt to speak in a sort of whispering mumble. If she was fortunate enough to have false teeth, the plumpers were affixed directly to the plate, so that the whole outfit could be removed with one motion.

If the arms were not plump or rounded, dress-sleeves were lined with wool or cotton padding in quantities sufficient to produce the desired result. Several Broadway shops did an extensive business in false calves, and in pads for sharp and angular knees, all complete with tape and straps. Large feet were made to look smaller by specially built shoes with the heels placed well forward. This fashion, called the "Spanish foot," was carried to such an extreme that the wearer of such a shoe, unless she was an accomplished toe-dancer, sometimes found it difficult to maintain her balance, and progressed in the manner of a rocking-chair. The "Grecian bend," which was revived in a modified form in the nineties, was produced by a complicated arrangement of bustles and pads and by the use of shoes with extremely high heels, which threw the body forward. Heels four inches high were not uncommon.

Corsets, procurable in every shape and color, were worn by all women of whatever station. Those intended for street and evening wear were heavily padded at top and bottom, and some had bustles attached. The lady who wished to display a particularly waspish waist wore a corset of special design and great strength. The ribs were of steel instead of whalebone, which had a tendency to crack under pressure, and the strings were of piano wire, guaranteed neither to stretch nor to break. Getting into such a garment was a difficult task, requiring the aid of two maids, or one husband, and was accomplished only after a great deal of hard work and considerable suffering. The lady clung desperately to two iron rings imbedded in the wall or the door jamb, while one maid pushed against her and the other tightened the strings, paying no attention to the gasps of the mistress. If the husband assisted, he shoved with his knee against the small of his wife's back and pulled the strings with both hands. A woman thus encased could scarcely breathe, but she was safe from the sudden breakage of corset strings or ribs.

While France was in the throes of the Franco-Prussian War—in 1870—the fashionable ladies of New York were wearing vast quantities of hair which had been cut from the heads of French peasants and worked up by American manufacturers into puffs, frizzes, chignons or waterfalls, braids, curls, rolls, switches, and wigs. Chignons, which were most popular, consisted of a framework of wire netting stuffed and covered with false hair and produced in butterfly, basket, curled, braided, puffed, knotted, and twisted patterns. They were worn at the back of the head, and some were as large as watermelons. Wigs, switches, and false curls were also in great demand, some women fastening as many as a dozen of the last to their own hair. Rolls and puffs were somewhat similar to the "rat" which formed the foundation of the more modern pompadour. They were made of short clipped human hair, or of horsehair, rolled and compressed over a small framework. The quantity of false hair worn varied ordinarily from two to eight ounces, but one very fashionable lady created quite a stir in society during the winter of 1869 by appearing at a party with sixteen ounces—about one hundred dollars' worth—piled atop her own luxuriant tresses. Once the false hair was in place, the head was deluged with flour, gold dust, or a glittering preparation called "diamond dust." Then the hair around the forehead was clipped or shaved, giving that in front a pointed appearance and sharply accenting the "widow's peak." Belladonna was rubbed upon the upper eyelids or dropped into the eyes, in the belief that it gave them a languorous and mysterious expression, and the eyebrows were either heavily penciled or painted with India ink, which produced a rather startling line of deep black. Some followers of this style painted a line above the eyes and another about half an inch long down either side of the face, so that the completed design had about the shape and appearance of the modern Dutch bob.

The practice of painting the face, neck, shoulders, and arms was extensively followed among the more extreme. Liquid and vegetable rouge were used in enormous quantities, as well as chalk, bismuth, preparations containing mercury, and various French pastes which came in small pots and were greatly favored by actresses and opera-singers. One cosmetic shop alone, in 1870, offered for sale thirteen different

A Belle of the 1870's

varieties of chalk and powder, eight kinds of paste, twenty-three kinds of face washes and lotions, and twenty brands of rouge. Practically every society woman carried a "Lady's Pocket Companion, or Portable Complection," which was very similar to the present-day compact. It contained rouge, powder and puffs, an eyebrow pencil, a small brush, and a small bottle of India ink. There were also many lotions and special paints for the hands, to which the fashionable lady paid much attention. The veins on the back of the hand were delicately outlined in blue, and the palm was painted in solid colors of great lustre and vividness, or in stripes, squares, circles, or other patterns. For several months during the early seventies it was very fashionable to color the palm of the hand to match the dress.

The women who really set the pace in New York during the eighteen-seventies were not content merely to paint their faces; necks, shoulders, and arms; they also had these portions of their bodies coated with a plastic enamel. This method of feminine ornamentation, one of the most extraordinary styles ever seen in New York, was introduced into the metropolis about 1868 by a chiropodist of lower Broadway, and at first all his clients were actresses. Enameling soon became popular, however, and within two years a score of studios were in operation, some of which advertised a coating that would last for a year, provided the lady kept away from a wash-basin throughout that period and used only the prescribed lotions and creams for cleansing purposes. Soap and water would discolor and streak the enamel, but would not remove it—only the proper solvent would do that. However, it is doubtful if anyone ever had a year's enameling put on at one sitting, and the claim that it could be done was probably nothing more than professional vanity and enthusiasm. Many society women made regular tri-weekly trips to the enameling studio, while a few had coats put on to last anywhere from a week to two or three months.

The preparation in general use was a compound of various ingredients, with arsenic or white lead as the base, and was worked into a semi-paste and tinted to simulate the glow of healthy flesh. A thin coat was applied with a camel's-hair brush, and one application was sufficient for one to three days, depending largely upon the weather. It hardened quickly, but if properly put on, the coating was too thin to interfere much with the natural play of the muscles, although the lady had to be a bit careful of quick movements or boisterous laughter. In their eagerness to exhibit perfect complexions, however, some women had the enamel put on very thickly. The enameled fair one was then proportionately pinker, smoother, and more glowing, but at the same time she was perfectly expressionless, for the slightest smile or quick movement was likely to crack her face. Enameling was not in any way comparable to the modern face-lifting; it was not dangerous, and its application did not require surgical or medical skill. Nor was it confined to the aged and ugly. For several years the style had a great vogue, but it was eventually abandoned because the flashier branches of society carried it to ludicrous extremes.

The process was fairly expensive, the range of prices depending upon the popularity and swankiness of the enameling studio. One application cost from ten to twenty dollars, but most of the studios would furnish a year's enameling at an agreed cost of from one thousand to fifteen hundred dollars. One studio advertised the following price list:

Enameling the face for one party	$10 to $15
Enameling the face and bosom for one party	15 to 20
Enameling the face to last from one to two weeks	15 to 20
Enameling the face and bosom for the same period	25 to 35
Keeping the face enameled for six months	200 to 350
Keeping the face and bosom enameled for six months	400 to 600
Keeping the face and bosom enameled for one year	1,000 to 1,500

"Plumpers" were from twenty-five to fifty dollars, including fitting and installation. False calves cost from seven to ten dollars; wigs were from forty to two hundred dollars. The "Lady's Pocket Companion, or Portable Complection," sold for two dollars, although jeweled and lacquered and engraved ones were manufactured to sell at much higher prices.

Over all these devices and all this intricate groundwork the belle of sixty years ago wore a dress so voluminous and bulky, and so replete with frills and furbelows, that several yards' clearance was necessary before she could navigate a ballroom. At the more formal functions the waltz and other so-called round dances were often eschewed because it was almost impossible for a gentleman to get close enough to a fair one to clasp her in his arms. This fashion finally became so extreme that a lady going to a really swanky party required a whole carriage to herself; no one else could squeeze in after she had arranged her flounces, bustles, wraps, and train and had tilted herself forward to protect her Grecian bend. Often the bend was so exaggerated that she had to lean forward and rest her hands upon cushions placed on the floor of the vehicle. Sometimes she was so trussed up that she had to ride standing, holding to straps attached to the sides of the carriage. Behind her in another vehicle rode her two dressing-maids, who held up her train as she swept magnificently into the house and up the grand staircase. Trains ten to twenty feet long were not uncommon, and many were so heavy and unwieldy that the ladies could not drag them along the floor without assistance. Some had long silken cords attached, and when a lady moved across the room a gentleman walked on either side, each holding a cord and pulling the train as if it were a cart. A woman thus burdened seldom ventured to dance, but when she did, a maid skipped through the intricate figures in her wake, holding up the train.

A great majority of these extraordinary outfits were made to measure in the home by dressmakers, for the ladies'-garment industry was in its infancy. They were trimmed and decorated with great elaboration and often cost very considerable sums aside from the cost of material. In 1869 George Ellington, who wrote a book called *The Women of New York, or Social Life in the Great City*, persuaded a "fashionable belle of the metropolis" to compile a list of her clothing and accessories, most of which had to be renewed annually. It took up twelve pages of the book and showed a grand total of twenty-one thousand dollars.

"We present it to the readers of our work," Mr. Ellington wrote, "believing that to the ladies it will prove interesting as a very faithful and correct account of fashionable female apparel, and to the sterner sex will serve to show how much the raiment of a woman of New York may be made to cost:"

Six silk robes—red, enamel, green, yellow, blue, black—with fringes ruches, velvets, laces, trimmings, etc. . . . $950.

One blue Marie Louise gros-de-Naples, brocaded with silver from the looms of Lyons; not a stitch in it . . . $300.

Silver bullion fringe tassels and real lace, to match . . . $200.

One rose-colored satin dress, brocaded in white velvet, with deep flounce of real blonde lace, half-yard wide; sleeves and bertha richly trimmed with rose-colored satin ribbon; satin on each side, with silk cord and tassels, skirt and sleeves trimmed with white silk . . . $400.

One white satin dress of exceedingly rich quality, trimmed with blonde lace and bugles; two flounces of very deep point d'Alençon, with sleeves of the same reaching to the elbows;

The Well-Dressed Woman Takes a Walk

bertha to match, with white bugles and blonde lace to match . . . $2,500.

One royal blue satin dress, trimmed apron-shape with black Brussels lace and gold and bugle trimmings; one flounce, going all around the skirt, of black Brussels lace; body and sleeves to match; sleeves looped up with blue velvet rose set in lace, to imitate a bouquet . . . $1,500.

One dove-colored satin dress, trimmed with velvet a half-yard deep; a long trail with the velvet going all around, with llama fringe and dove-colored acorns forming a heading to the velvet and going all up the skirt and around the long Greek sleeves; the sleeves lined with white satin and quills of silver ribbon going around the throat; lined throughout with white silk, having belonging to it a cloak and hood, lined and trimmed to match; made in Paris . . . $425.

One black mantua velvet robe, long train, sleeves hanging down as far as the knees; open, lined with white satin and trimmed all around with seed-pearls, as well as around the top of the low body; the pearls forming clusters of leaves down the front of the skirt, and all around the skirt and train . . . $500.

One rich moiré-antique dress, embroidered in gold from the body to the skirt and sleeves and all around, taken up and fastened with gold embroidery to imitate the folds and wrinkles of the dress; trimmed with white Brussels lace, with an underskirt of amber satin trimmed with Brussels lace, to show underneath; lined with white silk . . . $400.

One large Brussels lace shawl, of exquisite fineness and elegance of design . . . $700.

One crimson velvet dress, lined with rose-colored silk; train very long, trimmed with rich silk, blonde lace covering the entire train, being carried around and brought up in front and forming the bertha; sleeves looped up with white roses; turquoise fan and slippers to match . . . $400.

One blue mercantique dress (lined), low body, trimmed with Honiton lace; one piece of silk to match, for high body; two deep flounces of Honiton lace; handkerchief and cape to match . . . $300.

One sea-green glacé silk dress, trimmed with Irish point lace, flounced and black velvet bows and ends at intervals; Irish point lace on body and sleeves . . . $175.

One Irish point shawl, exceedingly fine; imported handkerchief and cape to match . . . $460.

One white moiré silk dress, trimmed with black point d'Alençon sleeves and body; large lace bars, crossed, all around the dress quarter of a yard deep, graduating to three-quarters at back; long train . . . $200.

One large black point d'Alençon shawl . . . $300.

One blue gros-de-Naples dress, with flounces of white silk, brocaded, trimmed with deep chenille fringe and blue passementerie; high body in the form of a jacket, with fringe and trimming to match—sleeves slashed and trimmed; low body, trimmed with chenille and silk blonde lace; bertha, sleeves and around top of body trimmed with narrow lace . . . $250.

One rich silk apricot robe, brocaded in white, not lined, with silk fringe woven on the dress body; trimmings and fringe to match; small cape for throat to match . . . $200.

One pink silk robe, with flounces; the flounces white ground and pink leaves trimmed with fringe; high and low body trimmed with fringe and ribbons; bertha trimmed with same; sleeves slashed open and lined with white satin . . . $200.

One rose-colored robe with flounces; high and low body, with fringe and trimming woven to imitate Russian fur; both bodies trimmed with fringe, ribbons and narrow lace . . . $250.

One mauve-colored glacé silk dress, braided and bugled around the bottom of skirt, on the front, around the band of Garibaldi body, down the sleeves and around the cuffs of Garibaldi body; the low body with bertha deeply braided and bugled, with sleeves to match; long sash, with ends and bows and belts, all richly braided and bugled with thread lace . . . $180.

One *vraie couleur de rose gros-de-Naples*, with flounces richly brocaded with bouquet in natural size and color, made to represent the same in panels, trimmed with gimp and fringe to match; also high and low body, with bertha and trimmings to match . . . $300.

One pink morning robe, very superb, trimmed down the side with white satin a quarter of a yard wide; sleeves trimmed to match and satin stitched; flounces in pink silk on edge of satin; passementerie cord and tassels . . . $250.

One gold-colored silk aerphane dress, with three skirts, each trimmed with quillings of yellow satin ribbon, looped up with pink roses; body to match, trimmed with silk blonde lace; satin quillings; silk blonde on sleeves, and lace and yellow satin; rich underskirt to match . . . $100.

Two very richly embroidered French cambric morning dresses, with bullion and heavy satin ribbons running through; one lined with pink silk, the other with blue silk . . . $100.

One rich black silk glacé dress, trimmed with bugles and black velvet . . . $200.

One blue-black Irish silk poplin dress, in Gabrielle style, trimmed with scarlet velvet all around the skirt; sleeves, body-belt and buckle to match . . . $125.

One cashmere morning dress, shawl-pattern; sleeves and flies lined with red silk, cord and tassels to match . . . $100.

One white Swiss muslin dress, with double skirt; pink satin ribbon running through upper and lower hems of each skirt; body with Greek sleeves . . . $90.

One straw-colored silk dress, trimmed with black velvet; body of same . . . $80.

One white Swiss muslin robe, with one plain skirt and one above; large and small tucks to imitate three flounces; sleeves with puffs and long sleeves with tucks down and across to match skirts; Garibaldi body to match; one pink satin under-body . . . $95.

One white Swiss muslin dress, with three flounces, quilled and tucked, with headings of lace atop each flounce; low body, with tuck, bretelles and broad colored sarsnet ribbon . . . $90.

One India muslin dress, very full, embroidered to imitate three flounces; Greek body and sleeves, embroidered to match sky-blue skirt and under-body . . . $110.

One India muslin dress, richly embroidered; high jacket and long embroidered sleeves . . . $90.

One pink satin skirt and bodice, to go underneath . . . $25.

One white long morning dress, embroidered around skirt and up the front; two flounces, one over the other; sleeves and cuffs to match . . . $60.

One white muslin, with white spots, skirt and bodice trimmed with bullion and narrow Valenciennes lace . . . $80.

Two white cambric morning dresses, one richly embroidered in wheels and flounces, the other plain; jacket to match . . . $275.

One white Swiss muslin jacket, richly embroidered, skirt and bodice to match . . . $100.

Three cambric tight-fitting jackets; collars and sleeves richly embroidered to imitate old Spanish point . . . $120.

Five Marie Antoinettes, of French muslin with triple bullion and double face; pink satin ribbon running through . . . $300.

One piqué morning dress and jacket, embroidered . . . $75.

One piqué skirt, richly embroidered . . . $50.

Six fine Swiss muslin skirts, four yards in each, trimmed with two rows of real lace . . . $55.

Two very rich batistes, for morning dresses . . . $120.

Two very fine cambric skirts, delicately embroidered, to wear with open morning dress . . . $60.

Two fine linen skirts, embroidered in open work . . . $40.

Two silk grenadine dresses, trimmed with Maltese lace and velvet; two bodices to match, in blue and green . . . $200.

Two silk barège dresses, trimmed with velvet and fringe; bodice to match . . . $200.

One Scotch catlin silk full dress, Stewart, trimmed with black velvet and fringe to match colors . . . $100.

Three Balmoral skirts, very elegant, embroidered in silk . . . $90.

One ponceau silk dress, trimmed with llama fringe and gold balls; body and sleeves to match . . . $250.

One blue silk dress, trimmed with steel fringe and bugles . . . $250.

One French muslin jacket, heavily embroidered, lapels and sleeves to turn back . . . $40.

One set of point d'Alençon, consisting of short sleeves, handkerchief, and collar . . . $120.

One point d'Alençon extra-large handkerchief . . . $100.

One set Honiton lace—handkerchief, collar, sleeves . . . $80.

One set Maltese lace—handkerchief, collar, velvet cape . . . $300.

One set Irish point lace—sleeves, handkerchief, collar . . . $80.

One cape of ditto . . . $35.

Two black lace mantillas . . . $40.

One black lace jacket . . . $15.

One Valenciennes lace cape . . . $75.

Two dozen very rich embroidered cambric chemises, with lace . . . $120.

Six ditto, with puffed bullions in front . . . $100.

Eighteen Irish linen chemises, rich fronts . . . $200.

Seven ditto, embroidered . . . $40.

One dozen night-dresses, rich fronts . . . $216.

Three linen ditto, very rich . . . $75.

One dozen embroidered drawers . . . $72.

Two very rich drawers . . . $50.

Eleven pairs silk stockings . . . $40.

One dozen lisle thread stockings . . . $20.

Nine pair boots and shoes . . . $45.

Three pairs slippers, embroidered in gold . . . $40.

One pair Irish point lace sleeves . . . $30.

One black velvet embroidered mantilla, imported . . . $450.

One ditto, embroidered with bugles, imported . . . $100.

One glacé silk tight-fitting basque with black zeplore lace cape, trimmed with narrow lace . . . $65.

One black silk Arab, with two tassels . . . $25.

One dust-wrapper, from Cashmere . . . $18.

Four magnificent opera cloaks . . . $175.

One red scarlet cloth cloak, trimmed in yellow cord . . . $12.

One cloth cloak, drab-color . . . $8.

One silk lined cloak . . . $10.

Two dozen cambric handkerchiefs, embroidered . . . $24.

One set Russian sable muffs, cape, and boa . . . $100.

One tortoise-shell comb, in one piece . . . $50.

Six fancy combs . . . $30.

One very rich mother-of-pearl comb, gold-inlaid, beautifully painted by hand . . . $85.

One fan of mother of pearl, inlaid in gold, with silk and white and Job's spangles . . . $45.

One blue mother-of-pearl fan, with looking-glass, imitation ruby and emeralds . . . $35.

Six other fans, various . . . $25.

One parasol, ivory handle, engraved with name, covering of silk and Irish point lace . . . $100.

Several other parasols . . . $25.

One real gold head-ornament, representing comet and eclipse . . . $100.

Twenty hair-nets, silver, gold, and all colors . . . $40.

Four ladies' bonnets, some exceedingly elegant . . . $100.

One box marabout feathers, for dressing the hair . . . $50.

One box artificial flowers . . . $15.

Velvet, silk, and satin ribbon for sashes . . . $35.

One small miniature model piano, played by mechanism, from Vienna . . . $50.

One writing-desk, inlaid with tortoise-shell and mother of pearl, lined with silk velvet; compartments and secretary; carved mother-of-pearl paper-knife, gold seal, gold pencil, case of fancy writing-paper, made in Paris . . . $200.

One bula work-box, elegant; inlaid with silver and lined

with ci-satin, fitted with gold thimble, needle, scissors, pen-knife, gold bodkin, cotton winders; outside to match French piano . . . $125.

One long knitting-case to match above, fitted with needles, etc. . . . $40.

One papier-mâché work-box . . . $5.

One morocco work-bag, ornamented with bright steel, fitted . . . $3.

One Russia leather shopping-bag, silver and gilt clasps . . . $15.

One gold filigree card-case . . . $20.

One set gold whist-markers . . . $50.

One small work-bag, silk fittings . . . $5.

One solid silver porte-monnaie . . . $19.

One little blue porte-monnaie, cords and tassel of velvet . . . $3.

One Ladies' Companion, fixings in silver . . . $45.

One hair-pin stand; a small book-case, with mirror . . . $14.

One basket of mother of pearl, gilt and red satin, full of wax flowers . . . $35.

One elegant Bible in gilt, edge mounted in gold . . . $30.

One silver pin-cushion . . . $23.

One elegant, richly carved work-table, from Mexico; three feet high, compartments lined with silk . . . $400.

One solid silver ruler, from Mexico . . . $25.

One gilt head-ornament, representing a dagger . . . $3.

One English dressing-case, solid silver fittings; of rosewood bound with brass and gilt, fitted and lined with silver . . . $250.

One pair ivory hair-brushes, engraved with name and crest . . . $155.

Two other ivory hair-brushes . . . $67.

One ebony hair-brush, inlaid with mother of pearl . . . $20.

One cushion of Berlin wool . . . $50.

One sewing-chair, elegantly embroidered . . . $75.

One fire-screen, decorated with beads representing Charles II hunting . . . $125.

One large sole-leather trunk, lined with embossed red morocco, handsomely ornamented with gold, with seven compartments and two large French patent locks; very scientifically constructed for the necessities of a lady's wardrobe . . . $250.

One traveling trunk, with cover . . . $73.

Grand Total . . . $20,900.

This list omits opera-glasses, without which the equipment of a fashionable lady of the seventies was not complete. They were sold in a great variety of designs and were very expensive. The finest in the New York of the period, and perhaps in the United States, cost $4,500 and were owned by Mrs. John Morrissey. They were made of solid gold, set with diamonds, and with a monogram wrought in pearls. Mrs. Morrissey was the wife of the famous politician who, coming to New York as a saloon bouncer and a gang fighter, finally became co-leader with John Kelly of Tammany Hall, and a member of Congress. At one time in his career Morrissey owned a palatial gambling-house on Broadway near the present site of Wanamaker's Store, and another at Saratoga. The latter eventually became the property of Richard Canfield.

CHAPTER 7

THE BROOKLYN THEATER DISASTER

AT EIGHT o'clock on the evening of December 5, 1876 the curtain of the Brooklyn Theater, in Washington Street near Johnson, rose upon a gala performance of *The Two Orphans*, which was nearing the end of a long and prosperous run. The title roles of Louise and Henriette were played respectively by Kate Claxton, one of the foremost American actresses of the period, and Maude Harrison. The remainder of the cast included such well-known players as Claude Burroughs, J. B. Studley, H. S. Murdoch, and Mrs. Farren.

The theater was of brick construction, but it was old and had been designed and built with no thought of fire hazards. There were no fire-escapes, and but four exits, all of which opened into Washington Street. One was a small door, at the end of the vestibule nearest Johnson Street, which was regularly kept barred and locked. Two of the other doors were each five feet wide. The third was much narrower. The only exit from the dress circle and the balcony was a single short flight of stairs into the vestibule. The way from the gallery led down a narrow stairway along the south wall of the building, thence round a sharp turn and down a long flight to the balcony floor, and then down a cased-in staircase and through the narrow door into Washington Street. Illumination was provided by open gas-jets in the lobby and the vestibule, and a few jets with ornamental globes on the orchestra floor. The footlights were simply kerosene lamps set on the stage behind tin reflectors. Similar lamps, called border-lights, were arranged in a row along the proscenium arch. They were faced with tin on the side toward the audience and were otherwise covered with wire netting. Above them dangled flimsy strips of decorative scenery, the borders, which invariably sagged into dangerous proximity to the flaring wicks. The dome of the building, which rose to a peak behind the stage, and most of the ceiling were covered with "parofile stuff," a variety of canvas which was extremely light and strong, but at the same time very inflammable. It was much used by builders of the period instead of plaster.

On the night of this memorable performance the theater was crowded, with the bulk of the audience—some six hundred persons—massed in the balcony and the gallery. The play proceeded without incident until the sixth tableau of the last act, in which Miss Claxton lay on a straw pallet while Mr. Murdoch, playing Pierre, delivered his speech. But he had said no more than a few words when a whisper of "Fire" was heard in the wings. Looking up, they saw that back-stage was heavy with smoke, pierced by flickering darts of flame. It was apparent at once that the borders had caught from the border-lights, and that the fire was spreading rapidly along the canvas ceiling above the stage toward the dome. Uncertain what to do, Mr. Murdoch stopped, but the audience had not noticed anything wrong, and Miss Claxton whispered:

"Go on. They will put it out. Go on."

Mr. Murdoch continued with his lines, and the scene was played through, Mrs. Farren, as La Frochard, and Mr. Studley, as Jacques, entering at their cues. The audience applauded Louise's defiance of Jacques—"I forbid you to touch me!"—but as she said: "I will beg no more," several blazing fragments of scenery fell upon the stage, and the actors were compelled to move. Miss Claxton's costume caught fire, and Mr. Studley pressed the flames out with his hands. By now smoke was billowing from the flies, and throughout the house men and women were rising to their feet and crying out in great excitement. Foreseeing the inevitable panic, the four players abandoned their roles and stepped to the footlights, while the orchestra in the pit struck up a lively tune. From one end of the stage Mrs. Farren and Mr. Murdoch urged the people to leave quietly; from the other Miss Claxton and Mr. Studley did likewise.

"You can all go out if you will only keep quiet," said Mr. Studley, and Miss Claxton cried: "We are between you and the flames! Keep cool and walk out quietly!"

Their advice went unheeded, for the conflagration had gained great headway. The dome was a seething mass of fire, and great streamers of flame, twisting in the draught created by the opening of the screen doors, were reaching out to the canvas ceiling in all parts of the building. Within a few moments burning timbers began plunging to the stage, and

Burning of the Brooklyn Theater

the actors were forced to run into the wings, while the musicians scrambled from the orchestra pit.

Meanwhile an alarm had been sent out from the First Precinct police station, which adjoined the theater, and telegrams had been dispatched to Mayor Schroeder and other city officials, but by the time the fire-engines were in position, the conflagration was beyond control. Fifteen minutes after the first flames had flickered upward from the border-lights, the whole interior of the building was ablaze, and the firemen and policemen who attempted to enter were driven back into the street by the heat and the dense smoke.

Occupants of the orchestra and parquet chairs, and most of those in the balcony, experienced little difficulty in escaping; they poured in an excited stream through the main doors into Washington Street, and through the small door, usually locked, which the chief usher, Mr. Rochfert, had forced open. But the hundreds in the gallery, at least half of them women and many of them children, had little chance from the beginning. Orderly progress through the tortuous passage was difficult under ordinary conditions; it was impossible for an excited crowd to accomplish. A score of men leaped headlong into the orchestra and were so badly injured that they could not escape. A few lowered themselves from gallery windows which overlooked an alley, and one man succeeded in forcing his body through a small rectangular ventilator. He dropped to the roof of the police station. Another man tried to clamber through this small window, but was overcome by smoke, and leaned against the sill until a gust of flame swept him away.

Only a very few of the people in the gallery could do anything to save themselves. Driven by the flames and smoke which swept against them from the stage and the ceiling, they plunged at once for the narrow stairs and went leaping and tumbling down the steps in wild confusion, trampling each other and piling in frantic, struggling heaps at the bottom. A few fought their way clear, but before any considerable number could escape the supports of the gallery were burned away, and the structure dropped into the roaring inferno of the orchestra. A few moments later, at 11:45 P.M., half an hour after the fire started, the wide east wall of the theater fell with a tremendous crash, burying the bodies of more than three hundred men, women, and children beneath tons of brick and debris.

The frightful scenes in the gallery were not visible from the orchestra, and when the newspapers went to press early next morning it was not believed that more than two or three persons had been killed. Some city officials, indeed, doubted that there had been any loss of life. Long before dawn, however, literally hundreds of people were clamoring at the doors of the police stations; members of their families had gone to the theater and had not returned home. About noon on December 6 the fire had been brought under control sufficiently for firemen and policemen to begin searching the ruins, and the bodies were soon found. Of all who had died, there was scarcely one that had not been hurled, by the collapse of the gallery, to within a dozen feet of one of the main-floor exits.

All of the members of the cast escaped excepting Mr. Murdoch and Mr. Burroughs. The latter hurried down from his dressing-room and rushed into the orchestra to help the people get out. He is believed to have been trampled to death. Mr. Murdoch rushed from the stage behind Miss Claxton and was never seen again. Some three hours later a New York reporter found Miss Claxton wandering in City Hall Park. She was dazed and distracted, her hands and face were terribly blistered, and most of her hair had been burned off. She was never able to remember how she had got away from the theater or how she had crossed the East River. That was several years before the opening of Brooklyn Bridge, and intercourse between Manhattan and Brooklyn was carried on by means of sailboat ferries and small, uncertain steamboats. A few weeks after the fire, before she had fully recovered, Miss Claxton

Ruins of the Brooklyn Theater

went to St. Louis with her brother and stopped at the old Southern Hotel. On the night of her arrival the hotel was burned, and again Miss Claxton displayed great coolness and bravery, saving her brother's life and herself running to safety down a burning stairway, which collapsed as her foot left the last step. The two fearful experiences almost ruined her career; for several years superstitious actors refused to play with her, and theatergoers of a similar turn of mind would not patronize the houses in which she performed.

The exact number of persons who died in the Brooklyn conflagration was never determined, but so far as loss of life was concerned, it was the most disastrous fire in the history of the territory that now comprises Greater New York. It remained the greatest theater fire in American history until the burning of the Iroquois Theater in Chicago in December 1903, twenty-seven years later, when six hundred and two persons were killed. The dead in the Brooklyn fire have been estimated at from two hundred and eighty to four hundred, the *World Almanac* and similar works of reference placing the number at two hundred and eighty-nine. Two hundred and seventy bodies were identified and given private burial, and the unrecognizable remains of many others, at least fifty and possibly a hundred, were collected and buried in a common grave at Greenwood Cemetery on a cold and stormy afternoon.

THE SAWING-OFF OF MANHATTAN ISLAND

ONE OF the most extraordinary hoaxes ever perpetrated in New York originated a little more than a hundred years ago in the fertile imagination of a little dried-up old man named Lozier, who had amassed a competence as a carpenter and contractor and had then retired to enjoy life. For almost two months during the summer of 1824 Lozier's fantastic activities, which he carried on with the enthusiastic assistance of John DeVoe, a retired butcher better known as Uncle John, kept a considerable portion of middle- and lower-class New York in a veritable frenzy of excitement. In later years Uncle John's nephew, Thomas F. DeVoe, an honored member of the New York Historical Society and himself a prosperous butcher of Civil War days, incorporated an account of the hoax in his two-volume work: *The Market Book, Containing a Historical Account of the Public Markets in the Cities of New York, Boston, Philadelphia, and Brooklyn, With a Brief Description of Every Article of Human Food Sold Therein, the Introduction of Cattle in America and Notices of Many Remarkable Specimens, et cetera, et cetera, et cetera.*

In those early days, when the Present American metropolis was a comparatively small city of not more than 150,000 population, a favorite loafing-place was the old Centre Market at Grand, Baxter, and Centre Streets. A dozen long benches lined the Grand Street side of the Market, and every afternoon from spring to winter they were filled with amateur statesmen, principally retired butchers and other such small business men, most of whom combined scant knowledge with excessive gullibility. Chief among them were Lozier and Uncle John DeVoe, and of these two venerable jokesters, Lozier was the leader. He did most of the talking at the daily forums in front of the Market and was invariably able to produce a definite and apparently practicable remedy for every conceivable financial, political, or economic ill. He was always listened to with enormous respect, for he was wealthy, he possessed more education than his fellows and was therefore better able to express himself, and he was a recognized traveler, having made several voyages to Europe as a ship's carpenter. There was no lack of subjects to talk about, for those were wondrous times. The first great wave of Irish immigration had begun to beat against American shores as a result of the potato famine of 1822; Brazil and Mexico had thrown off the shackles of Portugal and Spain; the first steamship had crossed the Atlantic only a few years before; President James

Monroe had just promulgated the Monroe Doctrine; and Mrs. Monroe had almost precipitated a revolution in New York and Washington society by announcing that as the First Lady of the Land she would no longer return social calls. The gifted Lozier professed to know the inside stories of all these momentous events, and so convincing was he that there were many who believed that he was high in the confidence not only of the President, but of foreign potentates as well.

Early in July 1824 Lozier was absent from his accustomed bench for several days, an unparalleled occurrence which aroused much comment. When he returned, he refused to join in the flow of conversation and even declined to settle arguments. He talked only to Uncle John DeVoe, and for the most part sat alone, brooding, obviously concerned with weighty matters. When his friends asked where he had been, and sought diligently to learn what mighty thoughts troubled his mind, he would at first divulge no information. At length, however, he admitted that he had been at City Hall in consultation with Mayor Stephen Allen. No one doubted the truth of this statement, which caused even more talk than had his absence. In those days the Mayor of New York was a personage of impressive dignity; he was not so approachable as now, and a man who had been summoned by His Honor automatically became a person of considerable importance. For almost a week Lozier kept his friends and admirers on tenterhooks of curiosity. Finally, on a day when all the Market benches were occupied and he was thus assured of an audience worthy of his talents, he made a full and complete explanation.

It appeared that Lozier and Mayor Allen had had a long conversation about Manhattan Island and had reached the conclusion that it was much too heavy on the Battery end, because of the many large buildings. The situation was rapidly becoming dangerous. Already the island had begun to sag, as was plain from the fact that it was all downhill from City Hall, and there were numerous and alarming indications that it might break off and sink into the sea, with appalling losses of life and property. Lozier and the Mayor had decided, therefore, that the island must be sawed off at Kingsbridge, at the northern end, and turned around, so that the Kingsbridge end would be where the Battery end had been for ages. The Battery end, of course, if it did not fall off in transit, would take the place of the Kingsbridge end. Once the turn had been made, the weaker end of the island would be anchored to the mainland, thus averting the danger of collapse.

When the conferences at City Hall began, it further appeared, Lozier and Mayor Allen were not in complete agreement as to the best method of accomplishing the mighty task. The Mayor thought that before Manhattan could be turned around it would be necessary to detach Long Island from its moorings and tow it out of the way, returning it later to its proper place. Lozier finally convinced him, however, that there was ample space in the harbor and the bay. It was at length decided, therefore, simply to saw Manhattan Island off, float it down past Governors and Ellis Islands, turn it around, and then float it back to its new position. For political reasons Mayor Allen wished the job to appear as a private undertaking and had turned the whole project over to Lozier, instructing him to employ the necessary labor and to superintend the work.

Such were the force of Lozier's personality, the power of his reputation, and the credulity of his generation that practically none who heard him thought of questioning the feasibility of the scheme. The few who were inclined to scoff were soon silenced, if not actually convinced, by his earnestness, and by the acclaim which had greeted the announcement of the project. Everyone realized at once that it was truly a gigantic plan, but they had Lozier's word for it that it could be accomplished. Moreover, as Lozier pointed out, the construction of the famous Erie Canal, which was then nearing completion, had once been called impossible even by competent engineers, and much derision had greeted the prediction that steam ships would one day cross the ocean. If man could run a river through the very heart of a mountain, and if he could cause a simple steam engine to propel a gigantic boat, why couldn't he saw off an island? Nobody knew the answer, and Lozier's story was swallowed *in toto*, hook, line, and sinker.

Sawing Manhattan Island off soon became the principal subject of argument and conversation at Centre Market, and elsewhere as news of the great project spread. Neither then nor later, however, did the few newspapers of the period pay any attention to Lozier's activities. It is doubtful if the editors ever heard of him, for in those days the only way of transmitting intelligence was byword of mouth, or by letter, which was even more uncertain. Important happenings in one part of the city did not become generally known for weeks or months, and frequently not at all. And Grand Street then was as far uptown as the farthest reaches of the Bronx are today.

A few days after he had started the ball rolling Lozier appeared at Centre Market with a huge ledger, in which he proposed to record the names of all applicants for jobs, pending an examination to determine their fitness. This and other clerical work which developed during the progress of the hoax was the special care of Uncle John DeVoe, who ceremoniously set down the names, ages, and places of residence of all who applied. Work was none too plentiful that year, and laborers, many of them recently-arrived Irishmen, answered Lozier's call in such numbers that the big ledger soon bore the names of some three hundred men, all eager to begin the great work of sawing off Manhattan Island.

Lozier further aroused confidence in his scheme by notifying various butchers of his acquaintance to begin assembling the enormous herds of cattle, droves of hogs, and flocks of chickens which would be necessary to feed his army of workmen. He estimated that he would require at once five hundred head of cattle, an equal number of hogs, and at least three thousand chickens. He was especially anxious to obtain as many fowls as possible, for he had definitely promised that all who obtained jobs would have chicken dinners twice a week. There was great excitement among the butchers, the immediate effect of which was an increase in the prices of all sorts of meat. One enterprising butcher had in his pens fifty fat hogs awaiting slaughter, and to make certain of a sale to Lozier he drove them north and penned them near Kingsbridge, where he fed them for almost a month at considerable expense.

With his food-supply assured, Lozier engaged a score of small contractors and carpenters to furnish lumber and to superintend, under his direction, the building of the great barracks which were to house the workmen during the sawing operations. A separate building, to be constructed of the best materials, was ordered for the convenience of the twenty or thirty women, wives of laborers, who had been employed to cook and wash for the entire crew. Several of these contractors let their enthusiasm get the better of their judgment and actually hauled a dozen loads of lumber to the northern end of the island and dumped them near Kingsbridge. They implored Lozier to let them begin building, but he said that actual construction must wait until he had engaged all the men he would need and had assembled all his materials. It was his intention, he announced, to muster his workmen at a central meeting-place when everything was ready and march them in a body to Kingsbridge. He assured the contractors that by using a new method of building which he had devised, but which he declined to disclose in advance, they could easily erect the necessary buildings within a few hours.

The excitement was now at fever heat, and Lozier added fuel to the flame by producing elaborate plans for the various appliances which were to be used in the project. First, there were the great saws with which Manhattan Island was to be cut loose from the mainland. Each was to be one hundred feet long, with teeth three feet high. Fifty men would be required to manipulate one of these giant tools, and Lozier estimated that he would need at least a score. Then there were twenty-four huge oars, each two hundred and fifty feet long; and twenty-four great cast-iron towers, or oar-locks, in which the oars were to be mounted, twelve on the Hudson River shore and twelve on the East River. A hundred men would bend their backs at each oar, and row Manhattan Island down the bay after the sawyers had finished their work, then sweep it around and row it back. Great chains and anchors were to be provided to keep the island from being carried out to sea in the event that a storm arose. Lozier gave the plans and specifications of these Gargantuan implements to a score of blacksmiths, carpenters, and mechanics, who retired forthwith to their shops and feverishly began to estimate the cost, and the quantities of material that must go into their manufacture.

Lozier now turned his attention to the unskilled laborers

whose names Uncle John DeVoe had set down as potential sawyers and rowers. He sent word for them to report at Centre Market for examination and announced that he would pay triple wages to those who performed the hazardous work of sawing off that part of the island which lay under water. The longest-winded men would be awarded these dangerous but desirable jobs. Laborers swarmed to the market, and every day for a week Lozier sat enthroned on a bench while man after man stepped forward and held his breath. As each displayed his prowess, Uncle John DeVoe timed them and entered the result in his ledger.

Lozier kept delaying the commencement of actual work by professing dissatisfaction with the estimates on the oars and towers and by insisting that he had not hired nearly enough men to do the job properly. At last, however, "the numbers became so thick and pressing," as DeVoe put it in *The Market Book*, that Lozier was compelled to fix a date for the grand trek northward. He hurriedly awarded the contracts for manufacturing the saws, oars, and towers and ordered them rushed to completion. He then instructed all who were to have a hand in the great work to report at the Bowery and Spring Street, where they would be met by a fife and drum corps which he had thoughtfully engaged to lead the march to Kingsbridge. The exact number who appeared at the rendezvous is unknown, of course, but DeVoe says that "great numbers presented themselves," and there were probably between five hundred and a thousand persons. Laborers were there by the score, many accompanied by their wives and children; the contractors and carpenters drove up in style, escorting wagons laden with lumber and tools; the butchers were on hand with cattle and hogs, and carts loaded with crated chickens. Practically everyone who had ever heard of the project was there, in fact, excepting Lozier and Uncle John DeVoe. When several hours had elapsed and they still had failed to appear, a volunteer delegation went to Centre Market in search of them. They found a message that both Lozier and Uncle John had left town on account of their health.

The crowd at Bowery and Spring Street milled about uncertainly for another hour or two, while the hogs grunted, the cattle mooed, the chickens cackled, the children squalled, and the fife and drum corps industriously dispensed martial music. At length, for the first time in weeks, if not in years, some of the more intelligent of Lozier's victims began to think, and the more they thought, the less likely it appeared that Manhattan Island would ever be sawed off. Gradually this conviction spread, and after a while the crowd began shame-facedly to disperse. A few of the more hot-headed went look-ing for Lozier, vowing that if they couldn't saw Manhattan off they could at least saw Lozier off, but they never found him. Lozier and Uncle John DeVoe had fled to Brooklyn as soon as Lozier had issued his final instructions, and had sought refuge in the home of a friend. There was much talk of hav-ing them arrested, but no one seemed willing to make a com-plaint to the authorities and so admit that he had been duped, and both Lozier and Uncle John went scot-free. However, it was several months before they again appeared at Centre Mar-ket, and when they did, Lozier found himself an oracle with-out a temple. The Centre Market statesmen had had enough.

CHAPTER 9

THE PERSECUTION OF THE REVEREND DR. DIX

ON A frosty morning in February 1880 the Reverend Dr. Morgan Dix, rector of Trinity Church, left his breakfast sausages to answer a ring at the doorbell of the rectory in No. 27 West Twenty-fifth Street. His visitor was a clerical gentleman, who presented a card which proclaimed that he represented a select academy devoted to the education of the female young. He had come, he said, in response to a note ostensibly signed by Dr. Dix, and was prepared to quote favorable terms for the care and training of the three little girls whom, according to the bogus letter, the rector wished to place in such an institution. Explaining that a distressing mistake had been made, the bewildered clergyman returned to his sausages, but it is of record that he never ate them, for scarcely had the clerical gentleman departed than another arrived. Thereafter they came in droves, more than a score calling before nightfall. And mingled with them were many representatives of Bible societies, religious and secular publishing houses, and all sorts of manufacturing and wholesale establishments, all of which had received letters saying that Dr. Dix wished to inspect samples and hear prices before purchasing large quantities of supplies for various charitable organizations under his control. And when no one else was ringing the rectory bell, the postman was clamoring for admittance with huge sacks of letters and post cards from firms which had not sent salesmen. Next day the procession of callers continued, and the mail was augmented by grave and sorrowful communications from leading Episcopal bishops and clergymen throughout the East, who had received curt notes, to which the signature of the rector had been forged, reprimanding them for not having answered Dr. Dix's letters. The tone of many of the letters from the bishops and divines was anything but Christian, and several hinted that perhaps the distinguished rector of Trinity should consult a physician.

On February 21, 1880 Dr. Dix received an anonymous letter, the writer of which said he would do his part toward making the rector's celebration of Washington's Birthday a memorable occasion, and that he had notified the old-clothes-women of Baxter Street and Park Row (then Chatham Street) to call at the rectory and negotiate for the purchase of Mrs. Dix's entire wardrobe. He enclosed a pair of soiled stockings which he suggested could be worn by the rector's wife after the sale. This time Dr. Dix arose early, and so was able to fortify himself with sausages and wheat-cakes before a rickety wagon, almost wholly occupied by a very fat woman and drawn by a forlorn little horse over whose back a small boy flapped the reins, rattled through Twenty-fifth Street and stopped before the parsonage. The fat woman descended by placing her hands upon the horse's haunches and oozing out of the wagon. Striding ponderously up the steps, she whanged the doorbell. When Dr. Dix appeared, she shrilly demanded that the clothing be produced, shouting that whatever the clergyman had for sale was worthless and that she would lose money on it. Dr. Dix attempted to explain, but abandoned the task as hopeless when another woman, with a sack over her shoulder, rushed through the gate and elbowed the first caller away from the door, while down the street a great clatter announced the coming of three others, who dragged hand-carts after them.

The rector retreated, slamming and barring his door, and the women settled down on the stoop to wait, convinced that Dr. Dix merely wanted to haggle. The old-clothes-dealers continued to arrive throughout the morning, and by noon the lawn of the rectory was filled with the excited clamor of twenty-eight women and twelve fretful children, most of whom were fighting, while the tumult was increased by the yells and gibes of street gamins who lined the picket fence and flung stones at the visitors. Several neighbors who attempted to enter the rectory and console the distressed clergyman were set upon by the women, who insisted upon bargaining for the clothing upon their backs. When one man refused to sell his elegant cloak, it was torn from his shoulders. Dr. Dix finally called the police, and late in the afternoon the women and children were driven from the yard by a squad of patrolmen.

But scarcely had the clatter of the carts and wagons died

away than a carriage whirled round the corner from Fifth Avenue, raced through Twenty-fifth Street, and drew up in front of the rectory. One of the city's leading physicians leaped out and dashed into the house, only to emerge a few moments later very indignant. He had received an urgent call that Dr. Dix had gone into an epileptic fit and was dying. Similar messages had been left at the offices of some thirty other doctors, and it was after midnight when the last of them had come and gone. Dr. Dix slept fitfully that night, and before breakfast was awakened by a half-dozen shoemakers who had been notified to call at the rectory and measure some children for shoes. Before lunch at least fifty men and women who had advertised for work appeared. They had received notes advising them that jobs were to be had from Dr. Dix. The afternoon was quiet, except for a large influx of mail, but about dusk a score of the most prominent clergy-men of New York presented themselves at the rectory, hav-ing received invitations, to which the rector's name had been forged, to dine with Dr. and Mrs. Dix and meet the Bishops of York and Exeter.

Next morning the business houses of Lord & Taylor, A. T. Stewart & Company, Stern Brothers, Arnold Constable & Company, and others received curt letters, also supposedly signed by Dr. Dix, saying that the rector had turned their impertinent communications over to his lawyer for immedi-ate legal action. Since no such communications, of course, had ever been written to Dr. Dix, officials of these firms were greatly excited and hurriedly sent emissaries to the rectory to assure the clergyman of their undying respect and esteem. This trouble had scarcely been disposed of when Dr. Dix received a letter signed "Gentleman Joe," who said that the annoyances would cease if the rector would pay him a thousand dollars. Dr. Dix was instructed, if he was willing to make the payment, to publish in the New York *Herald* two days later a personal saying: "Gentleman Joe: All right." This letter offered the first clue to the identity of the tormentor, and Dr. Dix promptly implored the aid of the Central Office, as the Detective Bureau was then called. The best minds of the police began to grapple with the problem, but none of the detectives knew anyone called "Gentleman Joe." Upon their advice Dr. Dix inserted the advertisement as directed, but in the same issue of the paper were two others exactly similar to it, obviously published by the persecutor. Gentleman Joe paid no attention to Dr. Dix's personal, but for the next few days he let the rector alone and turned his attention to a score of other prominent citizens, all devout church members and temperance workers, to whom he sent tart and threatening letters signed with the names of disreputable saloon-keepers and demanding payment of long overdue bills for beer and whisky. These insulting missives were given to lawyers, who collected many fat retainers before they were found to be bogus.

On March 17, 1880 Dr. Dix received another letter from Gentleman Joe, who said that unless fifteen hundred dollars was sent to a designated place, the rectory would again be besieged on the following Friday. Detectives took possession of the house on that day, and the clergyman locked himself in his office and refused to see any one but members of his family. Early in the morning there came to the rectory a lawyer with a letter to which Mrs. Dix's name had been forged, and which said that she wished to consult with him about a divorce. Twenty other lawyers called during the day on like errands, bearing exactly similar missives, as well as an agent for a steamship line with two tickets to Havana, and a score of persons who had advertised for lost or stolen property. They had been notified that their belongings were being held for them at the rectory. During the next three days at least a hundred persons appeared in response to summonses of various sorts, and about a week later an indignant stranger forced his way into the rectory, accused the astonished Dr. Dix of being too friendly with his wife, and threatened to cane the clergyman unless he immediately made a public apology. Next day the rector received a letter from Gentleman Joe saying that he had thoroughly enjoyed his visit, and boasting of his ability as an actor.

The police made extraordinary efforts to capture Dr. Dix's persecutor, assigning every detective on the force to the case and invoking the aid of the Post Office. Gentleman Joe had gone to the expense of procuring stationery engraved with "Trinity Parsonage, 27 West Twenty-fifth Street," but the printer could not be found; and the police also failed when detectives were stationed at mail-boxes throughout the city to open the receptacles whenever a letter was mailed and compare the handwriting with that known to be Gentleman Joe's. But it was not until a clergyman of another denomination mentioned that he had seen a former Trinity Sunday-school teacher who rejoiced in the elegant cognomen of Edward Eugene Fairfax Williamson that the police finally pounced upon the rascal's trail. They at once suspected Williamson because, having been unmasked as a person of low character, he had been expelled from Trinity when he scorned reformation and boasted of his amorous experiences in Turkey and other Eastern countries.

In the Post Office the police found a card upon which Williamson had written a request that his mail be forwarded to the Hotel Windsor, at Fifth Avenue and Forty-sixth Street.

His chirography was the same as that of the letters signed "Gentleman Joe." At the Windsor the detectives found that Williamson had left for Baltimore on the day his handwriting was discovered in the Post Office. He was traced to Barnum's Hotel in that city, and thence to a private boarding-house, where he was arrested. He told the police that he had not annoyed Dr. Dix through personal animus, but that he was impelled solely by a craving for amusement and had selected the rector of Trinity because of his importance as a citizen.

Upon his trial in New York he was convicted of attempting to blackmail the Reverend Dr. Dix and of accusing the clergyman of what modern journalism blushingly refers to as "a statutory offense." He was sentenced to Sing Sing Prison, where he died.

The police were unable to learn very much about Gentleman Joe's career and never knew whether he was simply a sneak-thief and a petty criminal with a tendency toward the sensational, or the equivalent of the modern master mind, and a thief and crook of unusual adroitness. They connected him with only a few petty thefts and swindles, and apparently he never worked, yet he always had plenty of money, and in both Pittsburgh and New York, where he lived during his two visits to the United States, he moved in good society. In New York, indeed, he became well known in literary circles, publishing considerable poetry and producing a play which was well received. However, it was later discovered that these literary works had been written by a nun in a New Orleans convent, though it was never known how Gentleman Joe obtained them.

Gentleman Joe first swam into the ken of the police in 1868, when he traveled extensively in Europe as an English gentleman and was involved in several minor crimes. In 1870 he came to New York, where he lived for two years, publishing his poetry and becoming a teacher in Trinity Sunday school. His only disclosed criminal exploit during this period was the theft of a quantity of gold pens, stationery, and other small articles from a shop opposite the Gilsey House, at Broadway and Twenty-ninth Street. After his expulsion from Trinity Sunday school Gentleman Joe went to Europe, and was next heard of when he was sent to Newgate Prison to serve a year for tormenting a Hebrew gentleman in London, in much the same fashion as he later persecuted Dr. Dix. Upon his release from Newgate, in 1875, he returned to the United States and lived in Pittsburgh for several years, swindling a few jewelry firms out of small amounts. He then came to New York and began annoying Dr. Dix. The police always regarded him as a very mysterious person and suspected that he was the ne'er-do-well younger son of a prominent English family and that he received remittances from his relatives. Apparently he had devoted his life to the commission of small crimes, not for the purpose of gain, but simply to amuse himself. His most pronounced characteristics while leading a comparatively honest life in New York were a fondness for notoriety and sensation and a great delight in writing letters. Of this last exercise he must have been very fond indeed, for during his persecution of Dr. Dix he penned more than three hundred, all elegantly phrased and displaying considerable education.

CHAPTER 10

BIG WIND FROM KANSAS

IN AUGUST 1901, when Carry Nation's spectacular efforts to hasten the advent of the dry millennium by wrecking mid-Western saloons and speakeasies with a hatchet formed the principal topic of conversation in New York bar-rooms, John L. Sullivan made a mistake. With his magnificent mustache quivering indignantly, the celebrated pugilist smote the bar of his saloon in West Forty-second Street with a ham-like fist and boastingly told reporters that "if that old woman ever comes to New York and tries to poke her nose into my business, I'll push her down the sewer." While the reporters doubted that Mr. Sullivan would be so ungallant, they nevertheless obligingly published his ultimatum.

A week or so later, on August 28, 1901, Carry Nation *did* come to New York. A horde of eager newspaper men met her at the railroad station, and the first thing she said was:

"Boys, I'd like to see this Mr. Sullivan. He thinks he's mighty smart, but I won't allow any man to push me down a sewer. Not while I've got my senses."

The reporters gleefully clambered into carriages, and with Carry Nation leading in an open barouche, they set out to call upon the famous John L. For this, her first visit to the metropolis, the smasher had characteristically arrayed herself in a black poke-bonnet with long white ribbons tied under her chin, a black alpaca dress over innumerable petticoats and what-nots, and a linen duster, belted at the waist. From her shoulder hung a satchel bulging with miniature hatchets, photographs, souvenir buttons, and sample copies of her newspaper, *The Smasher's Mail.* An enormous hatchet, almost as large as a small broad-ax, was stuck in her belt, but when she started on the ride across town, she shouldered the fearsome weapon, rifle-fashion, the better to protect herself against attack by the liquor interests.

Naturally, the cavalcade attracted considerable attention, and an enormous crowd quickly gathered when Carry Nation's coachman drew up before Sullivan's saloon with a flourish and a crack of his long whip. Standing erect in her carriage, the crusader loudly invited Mr. Sullivan to come out and take his medicine. Instead, a bar-tender presently appeared and said that Mr. Sullivan was asleep and could not be disturbed.

"Is that so?" said Carry Nation. "Then I'll come in and wake him up!"

Escorted by the reporters and as much of the crowd as could push through the swinging doors, the crusader rushed into the saloon. A newspaper man pointed out the noted pugilist, who cowered at one end of the bar with his face half-buried in a mug of beer.

"Mr. Sullivan," said Carry Nation, sternly, "put down that hell-brew and come here. I want to talk to you."

Slowly wiping the beer off his mustache, John L. stared for a moment at her embattled figure, then turned and fled. Carry Nation brandished her hatchet and started in pursuit, but Sullivan ran down the cellar stairs and bolted the door behind him. The crusader hammered upon the thick panels for a moment, but at length she became discouraged and shouted through the keyhole:

"All right, Mr. Sullivan! You wait! I'll be back, and we'll see if you'll push me down the sewer!"

A muffled grunt was John L.'s only response, and Carry Nation swept grandly from the saloon. Half an hour later the pugilist emerged sheepishly from his hiding-place and sought to cover his discomfiture with blustering talk, but he never quite succeeded in living down the incident.

Carry Nation invited the reporters to lunch, and the entire party clattered over to a Sixth Avenue restaurant, where the crusader was effusively greeted by a flashily dressed woman who said she wanted publicly to thank God that New York would now be rescued from the evil clutches of the Demon Rum.

"I believe in temperance myself," she gushed. "I really do!"

"If that is the case," said Carry Nation, coldly, "go home and put about four inches more of solid cloth on top of your corset cover!"

After lunch the terror of the prairies went to the Hotel Victoria, at Fifth Avenue and Twenty-seventh Street, where she registered as "Carry Nation, Your Loving Home Defender, Kansas." Turning from the desk, she espied a marble Diana in a fountain in the center of the lobby, and promptly covered her face with her hands.

"Look!" she shrieked. "She ain't got a thing on!"

She made such a commotion that the hotel manager hastily procured a large piece of cheesecloth and threw it over the statue, promising to keep it covered so long as Carry Nation remained a guest of the house. Thus pacified, the indignant crusader repaired to her rooms, where she gave each of the reporters a small hatchet inscribed "Carry Nation, Joint Smasher," and sang them a song which she had herself composed:

> Sing a song of six joints,
>   With bottles full of rye;
> Four and twenty beer kegs,
>   Stacked up on the sly.
> When the kegs were opened,
>   The beer began to sing,
> "Hurrah for Carry Nation!
>   "Her work beats anything!"

Neither on this nor subsequent visits to New York was Carry Nation officially greeted by the religious and temperance organizations which in recent years have practically canonized her; and the Prohibition agents who later imitated her destructive antics were then only a wild dream of the future. The rowdier element, however, had made great preparations for her coming. Most of the Times Square and Tenderloin saloons and beer-gardens offered special drinks named in her honor, and bar-room windows and mirrors were decorated with gayly beribboned hatchets and bore signs saying: "All Nations Welcome But Carry." Several saloon-keepers publicly offered to provide beer-kegs and whisky-bottles for her to smash, and employed press-agents to see that they received proper journalistic credit for their generosity. Others, fearing that she might damage valuable fixtures, hired guards to protect their property. Private detectives were stationed at every entrance to the Holland House bar at Fifth Avenue and Thirtieth Street, with instructions to keep her out by force if necessary. Had she ever got inside this famous resort, she certainly would have attacked the more or less pornographic picture, "Nymphs and Satyrs," which hung above the bar. It was the most celebrated saloon painting in the New York of the period and was said to be worth ten thousand dollars.

To everyone's disappointment, and particularly that of the reporters, who always gave her plenty of space, Carry Nation attempted very little smashing in New York. She was not only awed by the size of the city and appalled by the obviously vast extent of the liquor traffic, but she was afraid of the New York police. Friendly newspaper men had told her that the cops had received orders to handle her roughly if she became obstreperous, which they did at the first opportunity. On this particular occasion she was in the metropolis only a few hours, and devoted most of the time to bedeviling Police Commissioner Michael C. Murphy and Deputy Commissioner William S. (Big Bill) Devery.

About dusk she left to fill a lecture engagement in Ohio, but on Sunday, September 1, 1901, she was once more in New York and again stopped at the Hotel Victoria. She was greatly pleased to find the marble Diana chastely draped with cheesecloth.

"It's a good thing you covered her up," she told the manager. "I'd made up my mind that if that thing was naked when I got here this time, I'd use my hatchet on it."

A reporter, asked to mention a few well-known sinks of sin where a little Bible-reading might do some good, suggested the Democratic Club in Fifth Avenue, the resort of most of the important Tammany politicians of the time. Thither Carry Nation hastened, attired in a white piqué dress and poke-bonnet, and with a miniature hatchet glistening with bits of colored glass pinned to her waist, but carrying no weapons. She explained that she never carried a hatchet on the Lord's Day. She succeeded in getting past the doorman at the Democratic Club, but was stopped in the hallway by the manager and unceremoniously ejected, together with her reportorial escort. Leaving the Democrats to their fate, which she outlined in specific terms, the crusader took a walk around the Times Square district. At Seventh Avenue and Fiftieth Street she tried to follow several men into the side entrance of a saloon, but the bar-tender chased her into the street with a bung-starter, whereupon she cried loudly that she had been contaminated by the degrading touch of a liquor-seller, and hurried to her hotel to take a bath.

In the afternoon, attended by the reporters, she started on a tour of the old Tenderloin section. She entered several saloons in Sixth Avenue and berated the bar-tenders, and then went over to Eighth Avenue and hammered on the door of the Apollo Music Garden, a dance-hall and beer-garden, until the manager appeared.

"Bring out your women sinners!" she shouted. "Let me save them!"

"We have no sinners here, madam!" said the manager, slamming the door.

The crowd that had followed the crusader since she left the

hotel had been constantly increasing in numbers, and it soon became so large that Eighth Avenue was packed from curb to curb by a boisterous mass of men and boys who cheered vociferously as Carry Nation bustled from one saloon and dance-hall to another, crying the tidings of hell-fire and eternal damnation. Street cars and horse-drawn vehicles were unable to penetrate the throng, and late in the afternoon a policeman arrested her for obstructing traffic at Eighth Avenue and Twenty-eighth Street. Thereupon the crowd began to threaten the policeman for interfering with its amusement, and pressed so closely about him that in half an hour he had proceeded but three blocks with his prisoner, who added to the uproar by singing hymns at the top of her voice. At Twenty-fourth Street the policeman gave it up as a bad job and released her on condition that she return to her hotel, which she did after praying for him. She increased the general merriment by saying loudly that she didn't expect the prayer to be answered.

Next day Carry Nation went to Coney Island, where she was to lecture twice daily at Steeplechase Park. She made the trip on one of the old Iron steamboats, and spent the entire voyage trying to keep the waiters from coming on deck with trays of beer. They finally made their rounds in threes, one with beer and two with bung-starters. Thereafter, when they passed, she merely held her nose and saluted them with the 1901 version of the Bronx cheer.

The crusader was at Coney Island for ten days, and when she was not lecturing she was roaming up and down Surf Avenue and the Bowery snatching cigars and cigarettes from smokers' mouths, or annoying bar-tenders by leaning over their bars and asking loudly: "How many souls have you murdered today?" or "How is business in your drunkard-factory?"

A husky bouncer disarmed and tossed her into the street when she attempted to smash the fixtures in the Steeplechase Auditorium bar, but a few days later she made a successful attack upon a cigar-stand at the end of Steeplechase Walk. She smashed the show-case, and when the police arrived she was breaking cigars in half and throwing them into the crowd. She was immediately handcuffed, and when she refused to enter a patrol-wagon a policeman hit her with a night-stick, breaking a bone in her hand.

"God will strike you!" she screamed. "You beer-swelled, whisky-soaked, saturn-faced man!"

Later she wrote with great satisfaction in her auto-biography:

"In six weeks from this time that man fell dead in the streets of Coney Island!" (A policeman did die suddenly at Coney Island six weeks later, but he was not the one who struck Carry Nation.)

The manager of Steeplechase Park got the crusader out of jail on bail, but in police court she was convicted of disorderly conduct. Sentence was suspended when she paid the owner of the cigar-stand a hundred dollars. Her Coney Island engagement was not a financial success, for she staged such a good show outside the lecture-hall that few were willing to pay a quarter just to hear her talk.

Someone sent Carry Nation a copy of the menu card of Yale University Dining Hall while she was in New York, and she was aghast to see such items as Apple Dumpling with Brandy Sauce, and Roast Ham with Champagne Sauce. She promptly hastened to New Haven to correct this terrible situation, and visited the university campus under the guidance of an undergraduate club called the Jolly Eight. She tried to make a speech from the steps of Osborn Hall, but the students cheered so loudly that she couldn't make herself heard. When the President of Yale, Dr. Arthur T. Hadley, declined to interfere with the Dining Hall's culinary arrangements, the crusader hurried on to Cambridge, having heard that the Harvard boys were also given intoxicating liquors with their food. A thousand boys were peacefully eating lunch in Memorial Hall when she suddenly appeared in the doorway and yelled:

"Boys! Don't eat that infernal stuff! It's poison!"

A yelling mob of students rushed her onto the campus, but when she tried to address them from the stage of Randall Hall, they kept up a continual singing of "Good Morning, Carrie," a popular song of the period, whereupon she became enraged and scurried about slapping faces and screaming that Harvard was full of hellions. From Cambridge she returned to New York, where she expressed the opinion that both Harvard and Yale were nothing more or less than "schools of vice." This was on November 20, 1902, and that night she attended the Horse Show at Madison Square Garden, the swankiest social event of the season. With a swarm of reporters at her heels, she paraded up and down the aisles, shrieking with horror at the evening gowns worn by the ladies. She finally stopped before Reginald C. Vanderbilt's box and, pointing a quivering finger at his sister-in-law, Mrs. Alfred G. Vanderbilt, asked loudly how much of the Vanderbilt fortune had been devoted to the cause of temperance.

"Yes, yes," said Mrs. Vanderbilt. "Please write to me and it will be attended to."

"You ought to be ashamed of yourself for wearing such disgraceful clothes!" shouted Carry Nation. "Take them off and dress yourself modestly!"

By this time the Garden was in an uproar, and the crusader increased the tumult by alternately shrieking denunciation of society women and singing hymns as loud as she could yell, while the reporters crowded about Mrs. Vanderbilt and besought her to "issue a statement." Lackeys and attendants surrounded Carry Nation, but none knew what to do until Reginald Vanderbilt gave her a violent push. Then everyone pushed her, and she was hustled down an aisle and into the Garden Café, where she ran wildly about, overturning tables and smashing bottles and glassware. A policeman finally quieted her, put her on a street car, and told her she would be arrested if she returned to the Garden.

"I won't be back," she said. "Those half-naked women make me sick."

The hatchet-wielder was in New York a few more times before her death in 1911, but she never again attempted to attract attention or to rescue the metropolis from the thralldom of King Alcohol. She said she would leave that task to the Lord, and expressed the opinion that even He might expect some slight difficulty.

OLD HAYS

NEW YORK'S first real detective was Jacob Hays, more familiarly known throughout most of his career as Old Hays. He was born in 1772 at Bedford, in Westchester County, and was the son of a storekeeper named David Hays, who had been a soldier under George Washington on Braddock's ill-fated expedition against the French and Indians.

During his middle twenties Jacob Hays served for four years as a city marshal and at the same time was crier for the Court of Sessions and sergeant-at-arms of the Board of Aldermen. In 1802, however, his real life-work began; Mayor Edward Livingston appointed him chief of the day police force and gave him the resounding title of High Constable of the City of New York. He occupied the office for almost half a century, and became one of the best-known men in the New York of his generation. In those early days of the American Republic the Fourth of July and Evacuation Day (the anniversary of the evacuation of the city by the British, formerly observed as a holiday) were celebrated with elaborate parades, and one of the High Constable's most cherished privileges was to march at the head of the procession with the mayor, as a sort of official bodyguard. On these momentous occasions Old Hays shouldered a drawn sword and carried an ornate staff, while a flaming cockade decorated his hat, and his diminutive person glittered with badges and the insignia of his office.

The population of New York when Old Hays became High Constable was almost sixty-five thousand, but the police force was in an embryonic stage. The task of guarding the city during the daylight hours was entrusted to half a dozen city marshals and two constables from each ward, but these officers were primarily attached to the courts and spent practically all of their time serving summonses, warrants, and other legal papers, so that for some thirty years Old Hays was the only peace officer to patrol the streets from dawn to dusk. So vigilant was he that he never had more than six hours' sleep a night. The loosely organized Night Watch consisted of six captains and one hundred and forty men—about seventy of whom were on duty each night. The watchmen were paid eighty-seven and a half cents a night, and the captains a dollar more. These were not living wages, even in those days of cheap food and low rents, and most of the watchmen worked during the daytime as stevedores, teamsters, and mechanics. Since twelve hours constituted a day's work, they invariably came on duty tired and sleepy, and consequently were no match for the profes-

OLD HAYS ■ 115

sional burglars and other criminals who flocked to New York in great numbers from all over the country. Old Hays was appointed a captain of the Watch in 1803, but found it impossible to work both day and night and soon resigned.

For many years the watchmen were required, like their Dutch predecessors of the old Rattle Watch, to call out the hours, and the night was raucous with the bellowings of "By the grace of God, two o'clock in peace," and "By the grace of God, four o'clock and a cold, raw morning." Except for a thirty-three-inch club, they carried no arms, and wore no uniforms save heavy leathern caps, with an extension rearward to keep off the rain. Because of this extraordinary headgear they were dubbed Leatherheads, and continued to be so called until the eighteen-forties, when they were legislated out of existence, and the newly organized Municipal Police appeared on the streets with star-shaped copper shields. For some years thereafter the police were known as Star Police and Copper Police, but in time the latter was shortened to "cop," and became the generic term for a policeman throughout the United States. The old Leatherhead, however, had little or nothing in common with these elegant guardians of the peace. He was neither feared nor respected. Not only did the criminals regard him with contempt, but the young bloods of the town made him the butt of their jokes. They usually concluded a night of revelry by upsetting a watch-box with a snoring Leatherhead inside, or by lassoing it and dragging it through the streets at the end of a rope. This last was a favorite diversion of a young man named Washington Irving.

In the heyday of his career Old Hays was small, wiry, bald, and fussy, and walked with an amusing strut. Despite his posing and strutting, and an exaggerated idea of his own importance, however, he was one of the most expert thief-takers

Old Leatherhead

New York has ever produced. He is said to have known by sight and name every professional criminal in the East at a time when the country fairly teemed with lawbreakers, and his fame was so widespread that he was often consulted by the police of England and the Continent. Whenever a major crime was committed, the almost universal cry was: "Set Old Hays after them!" He went unarmed except for his staff of office, but he was very courageous and possessed great physical strength, and he was always ready to attack criminals or rioters regardless of their numbers.

Once while he was arresting Jack Reed, a notorious forger and cracksman, the latter attempted to stab him with a dirk. Old Hays gripped Reed by the wrist and twisted the knife from his hand at the same time pressing the forger against a brick wall with such force that three of Reed's ribs were broken. Flinging the criminal over his shoulder, the High Constable fought off half a dozen would-be rescuers and lugged his man to jail. Reed and two other men, named Stephens and Hollgate, were suspected of having forged several checks on New York banks. Old Hays arrested Stephens that same afternoon, after his son, William H. Hays, who afterwards became a broker and president of the Eighth Avenue Railway Company, had knocked a pistol from Stephens's hand. A few nights later a Watch captain arrested a man who said his name was Redmond, keeper of a hotel in Pearl Street. Redmond was identified as Hollgate by the cashier and the teller of the Union Bank and was placed on trial. The case against him had just been given to the jury when the High Constable walked into the courtroom with the real Hollgate, whose resemblance to Redmond was so striking that they might have been twins. Redmond was promptly discharged. His business had been ruined, however, and, sad to relate, he died soon afterwards.

Several methods of detection which are still extensively used by the police were originated and developed by Old Hays. He was the first New York policeman to shadow a criminal, and the first to administer the third degree, although such refinements as the use of a rubber hose and brass knuckles were thought up later. It was the High Constable's custom, when he thought a suspect whom he was questioning was lying, to crack the man on the knuckles or shinbone with his staff, meanwhile shouting angrily: "Good citizens will tell the truth!" Old Hays was also the first, so far as can be ascertained from existing records, to confront a suspected murderer with the body of his victim, a melodramatic idea which was subsequently adopted by the French police and became one of their favorite practices. The High Constable first used this scheme to extort a confession in 1820, while investigating the murder of a ship captain who had been found dead in Coenties Alley, near Water Street, with a bullet wound in his temple.

High Constable Jacob Hays

After a day or two of detective work Old Hays arrested one Johnson, who kept a sailors' boardinghouse in Water Street and had been notoriously active in shanghaiing unfortunate mariners. Johnson denied the killing, but Old Hays took him up to City Hall Park, where the body of the ship captain was lying in the Rotunda, a dome-shaped building which had been erected in 1818 by the artist Vandelyn for the exhibition of panoramic pictures. The body was covered with a sheet, and the room was in darkness. Johnson was brought to the side of the bier, and Old Hays suddenly swept off the sheet, at the same time flashing the beam of his dark-lantern and crying: "Behold the cold and clammy body of your victim!"

Johnson shrieked and shrank back, but Old Hays pushed him forward and shoved his head down until he stared into the eyes of the dead man.

"Murderer!" cried the High Constable. "Confess!"

"I killed him!" howled Johnson. "I killed him!"

He collapsed and was carried to jail. At his trial he repudiated the confession, but he again admitted his guilt upon the scaffold. He was hanged, in the presence of a great holiday crowd, on a special gallows which had been erected in West Twenty-sixth Street on the shore of Cedar Creek, a small stream which rose at Eighth Avenue and Thirty-first Street and, after devious wanderings, emptied into the Hudson at West Twenty-ninth Street.

A few years after this exploit Old Hays encountered and easily bested old Commodore Vanderbilt, who was as notoriously stubborn and "sot in his ways" as was the High Constable himself. The Commodore was commander of a steamboat owned by one Gibbons, and operated it on the Hudson River in opposition to the regular line, which was owned by Robert Livingston. In 1817 the state legislature granted Mr. Livingston the exclusive right to run steamboats in New York waters for a period of twenty years. He procured an order from the courts restraining Gibbons from operating his boat, and the High Constable went to the dock to serve the papers and take Commodore Vanderbilt into custody.

"If you want to arrest me," said the latter, defiantly, "you'll have to carry me off my boat!"

Old Hays promptly jumped aboard, picked the Commodore up in his arms, and a moment later dumped him down upon the dock.

During the first forty years of the nineteenth century New York was the scene of many riots and street brawls between the great gangs of the Bowery and the Five Points. Old Hays put down many of these disturbances single-handed, and employed a technique which for sheer efficiency and quickness of result has never been excelled anywhere in the United States. When he was informed that a riot or a street fight was in progress, he instantly repaired to the scene of the disturbance. He did not attempt to arrest the ringleaders immediately; instead he rapidly circled the jostling crowd and began knocking off hats with his staff, a comparatively easy task in those days because stovepipe headgear was generally worn even by the lowest ranks of society. Nine times out of ten a man whose hat has suddenly been jerked from his head will stop whatever he is doing to retrieve it, a trait of human nature of which the High Constable was perfectly aware. So, when a rioter stooped to pick up his hat and consequently threw himself off balance, Old Hays gave him a shove that sent him sprawling on the pavement. Within a few moments what had been a potentially serious riot had been transformed into the ludicrous spectacle of a crowd of men scrambling about looking for their hats. Meanwhile Old Hays had arrested the fomenters of the trouble and was marching them off to jail. Such a method might not be so effective nowadays, when hats are not held in such affection, but in Old Hays's time it seldom failed. It was never attempted, of course, during such serious troubles as the election and Abolition riots of 1834, which necessitated calling out the military. Whatever the extent of the disorder, however, the High Constable was never in favor of using troops, and they were always summoned over his protest. He was wont to say:

"If you send for the military, they may kill someone, and that will bring trouble; then there will be the trouble of burying them, and that will be the greatest trouble of all."

Old Hays's extraordinary activity finally enfeebled him, and after the organization of the Municipal Police, in 1844, he confined his work largely to serving court papers. He died in 1850, in the seventy-eighth year of his age, full of honors, and was buried in Woodlawn Cemetery. At the next meeting of the Common Council the office of High Constable was abolished, and the artist Shegogue was commissioned to paint Old Hays's portrait, which was hung in the Governor's Room at City Hall, where it still offers inspiration to the few city officials who ever heard of him.

THE WICKEDEST MAN IN NEW YORK

JOHN ALLEN, who was first called "The Wickedest Man in New York" in an article published in *Packard's Monthly* in 1868, was one of eight sons born to an industrious and well-to-do farmer of upper New York State, near Syracuse. All the brothers grew to manhood in the fifteen years which preceded the American Civil War. Two became Presbyterian clergymen, and a third entered the Baptist ministry, but the others hastened to the metropolis to seek their fortunes and soon went to the devil. Three were professional burglars and footpads, and another—Theodore—was for many years one of New York's most notorious gamblers and confidence men. Theodore also owned and operated, at various times, several dives and dance-halls, the most famous of which was the American Mabille at Broadway and Bleecker Street. He finally murdered another gambler and fled to South America, where he was himself killed a few years later.

John Allen was the youngest member of the family, and as a lad his conduct and disposition were such as to give his respectable parents good reason for believing that he was destined to follow in the footsteps of his clerical brethren. That his preparations for arduous labors in the vineyard might be the best obtainable, his father sent him to Union Theological Seminary, where he studied faithfully for several months. Then, convinced that greater material rewards were to be gained in other fields, and impressed by the apparent prosperity of his criminal relatives, he abandoned his prospective ministerial career and removed his belongings to a district more in keeping with his new ambitions. He lived and worked with his burglarious brothers for a year, learning the routine of their profession and doing quite well on his own account. At length, however, incensed by the regularity with which their movements became known to the police, they accused John of being a stool-pigeon for the detectives. He admitted it, and they gave him a beating and cast him out. In the meantime he had married a female criminal called Little Susie, who was well and favorably known in the underworld as an adept "lush worker"—that is, she specialized in robbing drunken men, or lushes, into whose liquor she first had the foresight to introduce knockout drops.

In 1855 or thereabouts John Allen and Little Susie repaired to the old waterfront district of the Fourth Ward—Cherry, Water, Dover, Catherine, and adjacent streets—which at the time was probably the wickedest area on the globe, a veritable cesspool of vice and corruption. There lushes of every degree of inebriation were to be found in great abundance, and Little Susie worked at her profession with much success, while John Allen became runner for a crimp, or keeper of a sailors' boarding-house. It was his duty to entice wandering seamen, or anyone else, for that matter, into the crimp's establishment, where they were plied with drugged liquor, then robbed and shanghaied aboard an outgoing vessel in need of a crew. Allen found this very congenial employment, and for nearly two years both he and Little Susie prospered. Then, in an unguarded moment, Allen took a drink with his employer—and awoke some hours later in the forecastle of a ship bound for South America. He had himself been drugged, robbed, and shanghaied.

Allen returned from his enforced voyage in about six months, and soon thereafter the keeper of the boarding-house was found murdered, beaten to death with an iron belaying-pin. The police found no evidence connecting Allen with the killing, but they suspected him, and he concluded to operate in other fields until the crime had been forgotten. Removing to the district around Sixth Avenue and Thirtieth Street, which in later years was to become famous as the Tenderloin, both Allen and Little Susie became associated with Hester Jane Haskins, a noted procuress better known as Jane the Grabber, who owned several houses of ill fame and supplied these and other places with girls. She employed a dozen respectable-looking men and women to travel through the New England states and lure young women to the metropolis with promises of jobs. Once in New York, they were abducted and forced into brothels. Allen and Little Susie labored for Jane the Grabber until she began to kidnap young women of prominent families, one of whom is said to have been a daughter of the Lieutenant-Governor of a New England state. Allen protested that this business was too dangerous, and he and Little Susie would have nothing to do with it. They resigned their jobs and dissolved all connection with Jane the Grabber. Less than a year later the procuress was arrested and sent to prison for a long term.

John Allen and Little Susie returned to the waterfront, and about 1860 opened a dance-cellar and house of ill fame at No. 304 Water Street. They also operated a gambling-house and drinking-place for boys in Cherry Street, where they provided small girls for the lads' pleasure. The Water Street dive was not far from a celebrated resort called the Hole-in-the-Wall, one of the few places in New York which boasted a female bouncer—an English giantess called Gallus Mag. Seven murders were committed in the Hole-in-the-Wall within a period of two months, one of the victims being a notorious gangster known as Patsy the Barber. He and Slobbery Jim fought to the death over twelve cents, for which they had murdered a poor German immigrant. Only a few blocks from Allen's Water Street place, also, were a low gin-mill kept by Bill Slocum; a boarding-house and saloon owned by Tommy Hadden, perhaps New York's most notorious crimp; and Kit Burns's celebrated rat-pit, where were held dog-fights, bare-knuckle prize-fights, and battles between terriers and the huge gray rats which infested the wharves. Both Burns and Hadden had formerly been leaders of the Dead Rabbits gang of the Five Points, and still commanded the allegiance of this choice aggregation of ruffians. Burns, Slocum, and Hadden figured, to some extent, in John Allen's later adventures.

In Allen's dance-house, as part of the permanent staff,

were twenty girls, very chic and handsome in scarlet skirts, low-cut black waists, and red stockings. Each girl also wore red-topped black boots, with circlets of sleigh-bells affixed to the ankles. As a sort of overseer, or major-domo, Allen installed a bruiser and gang-fighter named George Leese, also called Snatchem, who was described by contemporary journalists as "a beastly and obscene ruffian, with bulging, bulbous, watery-blue eyes, bloated face, and coarse, swaggering gait." This unwholesome thug kept the peace at Allen's house, strutting about with a knife sticking in his boot-top, two revolvers in his belt, and a bludgeon clutched in his huge fist, for in those degenerate days it was not against the law to carry weapons, concealed or otherwise. What time he was not working at Allen's Snatchem found employment as bloodsucker at the bare-knuckle fights.

Vice and depravity of almost every variety were always to be found at John Allen's house, which in all likelihood was the most vicious resort ever operated in New York. The things that were to be seen there upon payment of a few dollars defy description; moreover, even an attempt to describe them would fracture half the obscenity laws of the state and nation. It is perhaps sufficient to say that even along the waterfront they were considered pretty bad, although of course it was generally admitted that they were the sort of thing everybody ought to see once. It was after a slumming trip through the Water Street area that an industrious journalist named Oliver Dyer wrote the article describing Allen as "The Wickedest Man in New York," which was no misnomer. Allen was enormously proud of the title, and not only pasted copies of the article in his window and upon his bar mirror, but had business cards printed bearing this legend:

JOHN ALLEN'S DANCE-HOUSE
304 Water street.
WICKEDEST MAN IN NEW YORK:
Proprietor.

Dyer also dwelt largely, and with much regret, upon the fact that three of Allen's brothers were respectable clergymen, and upon the further fact that Allen himself had for a brief period received theological training. The article aroused much interest, and, always a keen showman, Allen determined to take advantage of his ecclesiastical connections and experiences. He began insisting that he was at heart a devoutly religious man, and announced that he proposed to surround his unholy business with a holy atmosphere, his ultimate object being the spiritual regeneration of the entire waterfront. He began to hold religious singsongs two or three times a week, at which he led his girls and the amazed habitués of the place in song and prayer, and himself expounded a passage from the Gospels. In every room of the house he placed a Bible and various pieces of religious literature, and every Saturday night he gave away New Testaments as souvenirs. He subscribed to the *New York Observer*, the *Independent*, and other religious publications, and on every bench and table was a copy of a popular hymn-book called *The Little Wanderer's Friend*.

The newspapers, especially the *World* and the *Times*, were very skeptical about Allen's professed ambitions to bring religion to the waterfront, but most of the city's evangelical clergymen were profoundly impressed, particularly the Reverend A. C. Arnold of the Howard Mission and Home for Little Wanderers, at No. 40 New Bowery. The Reverend Mr. Arnold attended several of Allen's meetings and urged him to permit an ordained minister to conduct them. At length, on the evening of May 25, 1868, the Reverend Mr. Arnold visited the dance-house in company with six other clergymen and as many laymen. Finding Allen drunk, they proceeded to hold a prayer-meeting, and continued to hold it until four o'clock in the morning, by which time most of their audience were drunk. Newspaper accounts of this meeting and of Allen's curious methods of operating a dive attracted large crowds of curiosity-seekers, and Allen's profits were enormous, as he promptly doubled the price of everything he had to sell. He now staged his exhibitions merely, so he said, as horrible examples of what formerly went on publicly in his house.

The Reverend Mr. Arnold continued to hold occasional meetings in the resort, and at length, after a long private talk with Allen, announced that "The Wickedest Man in New York" had been converted and was preparing to become a missionary. On the morning of August 30, 1868, Allen's early customers found the house closed and this notice tacked to the door:

THIS DANCE-HOUSE IS CLOSED

No gentlemen admitted unless accompanied by their
wives, who wish to employ Magdalenes as servants.

Regular daily services, under the direction of the Reverend Mr. Arnold and other ministers, were now begun in Allen's resort, and the following Sunday Allen attended the meeting at the Howard Mission and was prayed for by the congregation. A few days later the ministers invaded the dives owned by Kit Burns, Tommy Hadden, and Bill Slocum, who declined to make personal appearances at the Mission, but were prayed for nevertheless. By this time there was so much talk about the so-called Water Street revival that a statement to the public was issued, signed by the Reverend Mr. Arnold, seven other ministers, and Oliver Dyer, the industrious journalist. This statement said that Allen, Burns, Hadden, and Slocum had all been converted, and that the crowds at the meetings held in the erstwhile dives were composed of fallen women and other denizens of the waterfront.

These assertions were not contradicted until the *Times*, after an extensive investigation, exposed the entire scheme, declaring that the preachers had paid John Allen $350 for the use of his dive for one month. As part of the bargain, he had agreed to sing and pray and to attend services at the Howard Mission. The newspaper also showed that Burns, Hadden, and Slocum had each received $150 from the preachers for the privilege of holding prayer meetings in their dives. Moreover, said the *Times:*

"The daily prayer meetings are nothing more than assemblages of religious people from among the higher grades of society, in what were once low dance halls. . . . There are but a few, and sometimes none, of the wretched women, or ruffianly, vicious men, of that neighborhood present. Those classes have not been reached at all, and it is false to say that a revival is going on among them."

The exposures by the *Times* effectually put an end to the Water Street revival. Burns, Slocum and Hadden, incensed because they had been paid less than Allen, promptly evicted the ministers, and Allen's place was abandoned as a meetinghouse because the performances no longer drew large audiences. Allen reopened his dive, expecting a rush of sightseers, but, to his amazement, none appeared. Nor did the Water Street ruffians and the others who had composed his regular clientele return to enjoy his hospitality. They thought he was crazy and left him to his peculiarities. Allen operated his resort for a few months, but lost money steadily. His last appearance in the public eye was in December 1868, when he and several of his girls were accused of robbing a seaman of fifteen dollars. Allen was held for trial in General Sessions, but promptly forfeited his bail of three hundred dollars. He abandoned his dance-house and fled to Connecticut, where he spent his declining years on a farm.

THE AMBITIOUS SHOEMAKER

ONE OF the most famous of the old wells from which New York obtained its water during the first half of the eighteenth century was Comfort's Tea-Water Well in the vicinity of the present Liberty Street, a hundred yards or so from the shore of the Hudson River. Comfort's Water was much used by the rich inhabitants of that part of the city, who sent their slaves to the well with kegs, hogsheads, and pails, so that in time it became a popular rendezvous of the Negroes. It was, indeed, about the only place in New York where they could gather in large numbers without fear of punishment, for many stringent laws regulated their conduct. If three Negroes were seen together upon a public highway, each received forty lashes on his bare back; and if a slave was discovered with a club or other weapon, elsewhere than on his master's premises, he was likewise whipped. These and similar laws had been enacted during the excitement which followed the Negro Rebellion of April 6, 1712, when fifty or more slaves set fire to a house near the present line of Maiden Lane and then, hidden in an orchard, killed nine white men who ran to extinguish the flames. Soldiers from the Fort drove the Negroes into the woods and swamps east of the present City Hall Park, and next day all were captured but six, who committed suicide. Twenty-one were legally executed, and the remainder were flogged and imprisoned.

In 1741, some thirty years after the Negro Rebellion, the population of New York was about ten thousand persons, of whom at least one-fifth, or approximately two thousand, were Negro slaves. There were, in addition, about two hundred Indian slaves. Near Comfort's Tea-Water Well in that year, on the site of No. 10 West Street, was a low groggery for Negroes, kept by a shoemaker, a white man named John Hughson. With him lived his wife; their daughter, Sarah; a woman variously known as Margaret Salingburgh and Peggy Kerry; and a sixteen-year-old girl, Mary Burton, who had been bound to Hughson as a servant. The shoemaker's groggery was a favorite resort of the Negroes, and under his direction they formed themselves into clubs, called the Free Masons, the Smith Fly Boys, the Long Bridge Boys, and the Geneva Club, the last being the name of a brand of gin of which they were especially fond. Members of these bands, which were probably the first criminal gangs ever to operate in New York, stole whatever they could lay their hands upon and brought the loot to Hughson, who disposed of it and pocketed a major share of the proceeds. How many Negroes actually belonged to these clubs was never known, but the number was estimated at from three hundred to one thousand. So far as the old records show, the memberships of the organizations included no Indians.

Early in 1741 an English man-of-war brought into port a captured Spanish ship, and several Negro members of the crew were sold as slaves. They were sullen and intractable, and although often flogged, they repeatedly threatened to kill their masters and destroy the city. They soon began to frequent Hughson's groggery, and became the leaders of his bands of thieves. Almost immediately there was a noticeable increase in the number of robberies, but none of any great importance occurred until February 28, 1741, when several pieces of valuable silverware and a considerable sum of silver money were stolen from a house at Broad and South William Streets. Within the next twenty-four hours Mary Burton, who hated her master, confided to a neighbor that Hughson had often employed Negroes to steal for him. This information reached the ears of the authorities, who promptly ordered the arrest of Hughson, his wife and daughter, Mary Burton, the woman known as Peggy Kerry, and two Negroes, Prince and Cæsar. The slaves were accused of the actual robbery, and the others of receiving the stolen goods, which were found hidden in the shoemaker's attic.

Some three weeks later, on March 18, 1741, a wild and blustery day, fire was discovered in the Governor's House in the Fort, a little south of the present Bowling Green. Fanned by a strong southeast wind, the flames soon destroyed the building and spread to the chapel and half a dozen smaller structures, destroying them also. Then, in rapid succession, seven more fires occurred, and live coals were found beneath a haystack in a coach-house in Broadway. All of these fires occurred within a period of less than two weeks, all were suspicious, and one at least was obviously of incendiary origin. Nevertheless, New York felt no particular alarm until a Mrs. Earle, who lived in Broadway, told several friends that on the Sunday after the fire in the Fort she had seen three Negroes swaggering up the street in open defiance of the law, and had heard one exclaim gleefully: "Fire! Fire! Scorch! A little more mebby by and by!" She identified him as a slave named Quack, owned by a merchant. He was immediately arrested and tortured, but denied any knowledge of the fires. He said that he had been rejoicing over the capture of Porto Bello by an English fleet, news of which had just reached New York. He was unable, however, to explain why he had employed such unusual expressions, and so he remained in jail; and when a rumor spread that a slave had been seen to jump from a window of one of the burning houses, the authorities ordered the arrest of every Negro who could not tell a satisfactory story. Within a few days one hundred and fifty-four had been lodged in jail—and New York, always afraid of its Negro population, plunged headlong into one of the most sensational scares of its history.

Stories of every degree of wildness were soon in general circulation, and it was not long before the authorities began to hear vague rumors of a plot to burn the city and massacre the white inhabitants. On April 11, 1741 the Common Council offered one hundred pounds reward and a full pardon to anyone who would reveal the details of the supposed conspiracy, and Mary Burton, languishing in prison for her master's crimes, immediately told half a dozen different stories, in all of which she said that Hughson, the women, and the Negroes had held many secret meetings in the shoemaker's groggery, at which they had made plans to burn the city, divide the white women among the Negro slaves, and torture and kill the men. She said, moreover, that once New York had been destroyed, the Negroes intended to set up a new colony, with Hughson as king and the Negro Cæsar as governor.

Soon afterwards a white man who had been jailed for stealing property belonging to the Lieutenant-Governor gained his freedom by corroborating Mary Burton's story, though with some difference in detail. Both Mary Burton and the white prisoner said that the New York slaves expected aid from the Negroes of Long Island, who, according to their testimony, had formed a company and were secretly drilling with arms stolen from their masters. No evidences of such an organization, however, were ever found. Several Negroes, under torture, confessed to complicity in the plot, but repudiated their confessions when the authorities refused to release them in accordance with the offer of the Common Council.

Publication of these weird allegations threw New York into a condition of hysterical terror, and a few of the more timorous citizens promptly packed their belongings and fled into the country beyond Chambers Street, then the northern limit of the city. The panic was contagious, and soon a large part of the white population of New York, with vehicles of every description piled high with household goods, was streaming along the roads leading to the farms in the vicinity of the present Canal Street, and northward to the upper tip of Manhattan Island. In May the fears of the people were further increased by the burning of seven barns in one morning at Hackensack, across the Hudson in New Jersey, for which two Negroes were burned at the stake. As the torch was applied, one confessed that he had fired three of the buildings; the other maintained his innocence to the end.

Meanwhile the New York authorities were continuing their

investigations, and on April 21, 1741 a score of the prisoners were brought to trial in the Supreme Court. On Mary Burton's evidence alone Hughson, his wife and daughter, Peggy Kerry, and the Negroes Prince and Cæsar were quickly convicted. Hughson's daughter was eventually pardoned on condition that she leave New York, but sentence of death was pronounced upon the others by the Chief Justice, who thus addressed the shoemaker:

"Thou vile wretch! Your hypocritical, canting behavior upon your trial, your protestations of innocence, your dissimulation before God and man, will be no small article against you at the Day of Judgment. For what saith the Word? They that have done evil and die impenitent shall be thrown into the infernal lake of fire and brimstone, together with the Devil and his accursed spirits, where the worm never dieth and the fire will never be quenched. In this torment you must remain under the most bitter weeping, wailing and gnashing of teeth, time without end."

The executions began on May 11, 1741, when Prince and Cæsar were hanged in the presence of several thousand excited citizens, many of whom had returned to the city for the occasion. Hughson was repeatedly urged to confess, but insisted that he knew nothing of the conspiracy, and said that he did not doubt that some remarkable sign would be forthcoming to prove his innocence. When he was taken in a cart to the scene of execution at the Battery, he stood all the way, pointing toward Heaven with one finger, as if to summon the celestial hosts to his assistance. But the expected miracle failed to materialize, and he was duly hanged on June 12, together with his wife and Peggy Kerry. After their deaths both Hughson and the Negro Cæsar were hung in chains on a gibbet, a sort of gallows without a trap, upon which executed criminals were displayed as a noisome warning to evil-doers.

During the week that followed the 12th of June, more than a dozen Negroes were convicted and hanged. Two were burned at stakes set fifty feet apart near the present site of City Hall Park, then a meadow, and several others died in the flames a hundred yards farther north, near the present City Hall Place.

On June 19, 1741 a pardon was again offered to all who would confess, and Mary Burton made her position even more secure by suddenly remembering that John Ury, a Catholic school-teacher, had been involved in the plot. She testified that she had often seen him at Hughson's groggery in conference with the shoemaker and the Negroes, and that she had heard him urge the slaves to burn every house in New York. Ury was arrested, and tried not only for engaging in the conspiracy, but also for officiating as a priest in violation of a law passed in 1700 to drive the French missionaries out of the Indian country. The evidence against him was slight, but the judges were greatly impressed by a letter from General Oglethorpe, who had written from Georgia that the Spaniards had planned to destroy every English town on the American continent and had employed many Catholic priests to assist in the scheme. Ury was soon convicted, and was hanged on August 29, 1741.

He was the last person to be executed. Emboldened by her successes, Mary Burton began to make absurd accusations against various persons of consequence, and even declared that some of the judges of the Supreme Court, as well as other colonial and municipal officials, had been boon companions of Hughson and the Negroes. Such charges were obviously preposterous, and both the people and the authorities began to realize that none of the evidence upon which so many persons had been sent to their deaths had been conclusive, and that in all likelihood the conspiracy had never existed save in the fertile imagination of Mary Burton. Within a short time after the hanging of Ury the investigation was abandoned and the prisoners who remained in jail were released. But enough mischief had already been done—four white persons had been hanged, and twenty others had been imprisoned; fourteen Negroes had been burned at the stake, twenty had been hanged, and seventy-one had been transported to other colonies.

CHAPTER 14

THE GREAT FIRE OF 1835

WHEN DARKNESS fell upon New York on Wednesday, December 16, 1835, the metropolis settled grimly down to endure one of the coldest nights within the memory of the oldest inhabitant. The thermometer, which had been hovering between twelve and fifteen degrees below zero for several days, had dropped to seventeen, and from the northwest roared an icy gale that whistled threateningly in the eaves and rocked the smaller buildings until they tottered on their foundations. Upon the sidewalks and pavements lay two feet of closely packed snow; it had been falling steadily for twenty-four hours. The Hudson River was frozen, and so was the East River except for a narrow channel; the wells, cisterns, and reservoirs contained nothing but solid blocks of ice, and only a tiny trickle flowed sluggishly in the ice-choked logs by which water was piped through the lower half of the city. Water was the scarcest commodity in New York; the men who ordinarily peddled it from carts had been driven from the streets by the cold and the snow, and even the richest citizens were compelled to lug home cakes of ice and melt them in their ovens.

A few minutes after nine o'clock a private watchman employed by the insurance companies saw smoke floating from a window of a five-story structure at 25 Merchant Street, now a part of Hanover Street. Unable to enter the building, the watchman ran through the streets crying for help, and within a few minutes the great bell in the cupola of City Hall had loosed its brazen clamor into the storm. Other stations quickly took up the alarm, and soon the city was filled with the frenzied ringing of bells, and the hoarse shouting of excited men as the firemen pushed and pulled their engines and other apparatus through the deep snow. But in less than half an hour, long before the first feeble stream of water had splashed upon the flames, the fire had spread to Water Street and Exchange Place, destroying the buildings on both sides of Old and Coenties Slips, and thence to Beaver, Front, and South Streets. By midnight the conflagration was raging fiercely in a rectangular area some thirteen acres in extent and including seventeen blocks bounded, roughly, by Coenties Slip and Broad, Wall, and South Streets. This was the financial and business heart of New York, containing the banks, the insurance offices, the Merchants' Exchange (the stock exchange of the period), many dwellings and factories, several churches, most of the newspaper plants, and the most important of the retail and wholesale stores and warehouses. The crowded shipping in the East River was also endangered, but fortunately the channel was open, and the vessels were saved by being moved into the middle of the stream. One ship, a brig, caught fire, but the flames were extinguished by members of her crew.

The Great Fire of 1835

Every fire company in New York had answered the alarm, and within two hours after the fire had been discovered more than seventy-five engines, hose-carts, and hook-and-ladder trucks were on the scene, while hundreds of citizens had brought buckets, pails, and tubs. But most of the apparatus was useless. The thin streams that came from the hydrants would not throw more than thirty feet, and they were so feeble that the wind blew them back against the firemen who held the hose-pipes, quickly coating the men with ice. Additional water could be obtained only by melting the cisterns and wells and by chopping through the ice at the ends of piers and docks. Almost as rapidly as water was pumped into the hose, it froze and impeded the flow, and if an engine stopped working for more than a few seconds, the machinery froze so solid that it could not be started again without breaking some essential part of the mechanism. Several engines were lowered off the docks onto the ice and worked from that vantage point, and Black Joke Engine No. 33 was dragged onto the deck of a ship, and from there pumped water through three other engines and finally into the fire in Wall Street. The men of Black Joke labored at their machine for five hours and then stopped to rest. A moment later the engine was so frozen that it could not be operated. The other engines were destroyed by fires built under them to thaw them out.

Two structures, the Journal of Commerce building in Garden Street and the restaurant operated by Downing, the Oyster King, in Broad Street, were saved by the use of vinegar, great casks of which were rolled out of Downing's place and poured into an engine, which pumped it on the flames. But the supply was soon exhausted, and realizing that they could not obtain sufficient water or other liquid to accomplish anything, the firemen turned their attention to saving property. At first it did not seem likely that the flames would reach Hanover Square, and in that apparently safe area were heaped great piles of valuable merchandise, including silks, satins, laces, baskets of champagne, and cases of wine and fine tea. About an hour after midnight, however, the warehouse of Peter Remsen & Company, on the southeast corner of the square, burst into flames, and a gust of wind blew burning embers into the piles of goods. They were destroyed before anyone could rescue them.

Many merchants carried their stocks into the Dutch Reformed Church in Garden Street, and into the Merchants' Exchange, which was on the south side of Wall Street, between William and Hanover Streets, and extended rearward to Exchange Place. Both buildings were eventually burned.

The Exchange did not catch fire until two o'clock in the morning of Thursday, December 17. Half a dozen sailors, members of a detachment sent from the Navy Yard, carried out a large quantity of merchandise and also attempted to save a marble statue of Alexander Hamilton, which stood in the rotunda of the building. They were removing it from the pedestal when a warning cry was raised that the structure was about to collapse, and they fled into the street just in time to escape being buried in the ruins. Within another hour the church in Garden Street was also in flames, and the fire spread so rapidly that none of the property which had been stored in it could be saved. Soon after the edifice was discovered to be on fire, someone began playing a funeral dirge upon the church organ. The solemn strains soared high above the roar of the flames and the shouts of the firemen, stopping suddenly in the middle of a bar when the building collapsed. The identity of the musician was never learned.

Hour after hour the fire roared and crackled, while the lower half of Manhattan Island was enveloped in a billowing cloak of dense black smoke, pierced by groping ribbons of flame that reached high into the heavens. The illumination was so great against the sky that it was visible a hundred miles away, and from the Long Island and New Jersey shores the metropolis appeared to be one vast sheet of flame. Throughout the night the wind continued to blow with the violence of a gale, carrying burning embers across the East River and depositing them as far inland as Joralemon Street, Brooklyn.

Many of the buildings in the burning area were new structures covered with iron or copper roofing, and the heat soon became so great that the metals melted and poured off the roofs in fiery rivulets, further endangering the firemen. One of the stores facing Hanover Square contained a large quantity of sheet lead, which melted and ran together in such huge masses that the owner, when the fire had subsided, was obliged to quarry it out. Despite the terrific heat, however, the cold a few yards away from the fire was so intense that scores of firemen hobbled about with frozen toes, fingers, and ears.

The conflagration, by far the most devastating that has ever occurred in New York, threw the entire city into a ferment of excitement. Crowds that seriously hampered the work of the firemen surged back and forth through the downtown streets, while from the rookeries of the Five Points and other slum districts came hordes of rowdies, hoodlums, and criminals, attended by their wives, sweethearts, and children. They immediately plunged into a saturnalia of looting, which continued almost without interruption for twenty-four hours, when the devastated area was placed under martial law and patrolled by marines from the Navy Yard and by the Third and Ninth militia regiments. Cases and kegs of wines and liquors were smashed and their contents greedily drunk; after the fire it was estimated that ten thousand bottles of champagne alone had been consumed by the mobs which swarmed about the streets, stealing and fighting. Men and women swaggered about with their rags hidden beneath rich cloaks, frock coats, and plug hats and silks and satins of the finest quality; scores returned to their dens at the Five Points laden with great bundles of clothing and valuable property of every description. Half a dozen men, apparently frenzied by the unparalleled opportunity for thieving, were caught by the police trying to set fire to houses beyond the burning district. One man who was discovered applying the torch to a building at Stone and Broad Streets was promptly hanged to a tree by a group of irate citizens. His body, frozen stiff, dangled for three days before the police found time to cut it down.

By four o'clock on Thursday morning, December 17, it was apparent that only the most heroic measures could save the entire city from destruction. Mayor Cornelius W. Lawrence, after consultation with other city officials, decided to blow up buildings at various points and create gaps which it was hoped the flames could not cross. However, once this decision had been made, a new difficulty arose. The sale of powder was forbidden in New York, and enough for the purpose could not be found in the city, while only a few pounds were stored at the army post on Governors Island. At length a barge was dispatched from the Navy Yard to the naval magazine at Red Hook, now a part of Brooklyn, for a supply of the explosive. It arrived at dawn, in the custody of eighty marines and a dozen sailors. The demolition of the buildings was begun immediately, but it was not until noon that the necessary break was made at Coenties Slip by the destruction of a building occupied by a firm of wholesale grocers. The southward progress of the conflagration was then checked, and what remained of New York had been saved.

On the day following the fire, business was wholly suspended, and for a while it seemed that the metropolis had been dealt a blow from which it would never recover. Thousands gathered in silent crowds about the great heaps of ruins which blocked the downtown streets, and merchants and their clerks stood weeping beside the pitiful remnants of their stocks of goods. Scarcely a building remained standing in South Front, Pearl, Stone, Beaver, Water, Merchant, Hanover, and other important streets, while, with the exception of five houses, the south side of Wall Street had been destroyed from William to South Street. According to the computation of the *Courier & Enquirer*, one of the two morning papers which escaped the destruction, six hundred and seventy-four build-

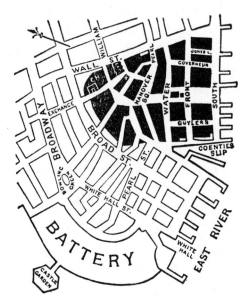

The Great Fire of 1835. The burned district in black.
"X" Shows where the fire started.

ings were burned. Other accounts give different figures, ranging upward from five hundred and twenty-eight. The loss was
estimated at from twenty million dollars to twenty-five million dollars, which, in comparison with the wealth and population of the city, would be equivalent to a modern loss of
almost half a billion dollars. The amount of insurance in
effect was about ten million dollars, little of which was ever
paid, for the disaster was so overwhelming that most of the
insurance companies and banks were compelled to suspend
operations. Arthur Tappan, a prominent Abolitionist and a
silk-merchant, who with his brother Lewis founded the *Journal of Commerce*, is said to have fared better than any other
business man whose establishment was in the burned area.
His store was a stone building at 122 Pearl Street. Soon after

the Abolition riots of 1834, when his place was attacked by mobs, he had equipped his windows with shutters of thick boiler iron, which resisted the flames long enough for one hundred thousand dollars' worth of merchandise to be carried into the street. Most of Tappan's goods were saved by Negroes whom he had befriended. New York insurance offices would not write policies on Tappan's property because he was an Abolitionist, but from Boston companies he had obtained insurance amounting to about three hundred thousand dollars, all of which was paid.

Many rumors that the great fire was of incendiary origin were afloat, but none was ever verified. The authorities finally decided that it had been caused by the explosion of a gas-pipe in the house at 25 Merchant Street.

CHAPTER 15

THE ESCAPE OF WILLIAM J. SHARKEY

WILLIAM J. SHARKEY, burglar, pickpocket, Tammany heeler during the palmy days of William M. Tweed, and captain of a fighting gang called the Sharkey Guards, went to Buffalo during the summer of 1872 and started a faro bank. He was unlucky, lost four thousand dollars in five days, and returned to New York, where he met his friend Robert Dunn, alias Bob Isaacs, an employee of the City Comptroller's office and a faro dealer in a Fulton Street gambling-house. Sharkey engaged Dunn to operate the game in Buffalo and advanced him six hundred dollars, which Dunn agreed to repay. But Dunn was also unlucky and came back to the metropolis late in August 1872. On September 1, which was Sunday, both he and Sharkey attended the funeral of James Reilly, a prominent member of the Michael Norton Association, a Tammany political organization. From the cemetery they went, separately, to Charles Harvey's saloon, The Place, at 288 Hudson Street.

Dunn arrived first and was drinking rye whisky at the bar when Sharkey entered. Sharkey had a drink and then asked Dunn to return the six hundred dollars. Dunn replied that he hadn't any money. Sharkey became furiously angry. Drawing a single-barreled derringer pistol, he backed away and pointed it at Dunn, who cried:

William J. Sharkey

"Don't shoot, Billy! I'll pay you as soon as I can!"

"You'd better pay me now!" shouted Sharkey.

He pulled the trigger, and when the smoke lifted, Dunn lay dead upon the floor, with a bullet in his heart. Sharkey fled from the saloon, but was captured by the police a few hours later in a house in Washington Street, near Perry. The wheels of justice turned slowly, and Sharkey was not brought to trial until the summer of 1873. A jury in the Court of General Sessions, with Recorder Hackett presiding, found him guilty of murder in the first degree. On July 3, 1873, he was sentenced to be hanged on August 15. The Supreme Court promptly granted a writ of error, however, which operated as a stay of execution, and Sharkey was sent to the Tombs to await the action of the higher tribunal.

Sharkey had a sweetheart—the police records intimate that she may have been his wife—named Maggie Jourdan. Her parents were respectable people of the Ninth Ward, but she herself had been an associate of criminals since early girlhood. Before she became infatuated with Sharkey, she consorted with Thomas Murphy, a pickpocket, and became a very skillful thief. She was an intimate friend of Mrs. Wesley Allen, wife of a burglar whose brother John Allen operated a low dance-house in Water Street and was known as "The Wickedest Man in New York."

Maggie Jourdan visited Sharkey every day during his incarceration—admission to the Tombs was by pass issued at the prison entrance—and sat for several hours in front of his cell or strolled with him through the corridors. Because of the activities of the Tweed Ring, practically every department of the city government was thoroughly demoralized and graft-ridden. The Tombs was no exception. The prison was administered with an extraordinary lack of discipline. While ordinary criminals were confined in dark cells and harshly treated, those with money or influential political connections occupied the large and airy cells on the second tier, called Murderers' Row, the doors of which were seldom locked. They had many privileges and liberties which would be accounted unusual even in this modern age of coddling and

Murderers' Row in the Tombs

sentimentality. Sharkey was never permitted to leave the prison, because he was under sentence of death, but otherwise he fared better than most, for Maggie Jourdan picked pockets industriously, sold her dresses and jewelry, and spent the proceeds for his comfort. She bought him a handsome walnut table, a Kidderminster carpet, a canary in a cage, a book-and-magazine rack which was suspended from the ceiling by silken cords, a soft mattress for his bed, a patent extension chair for lounging, draperies for the cell door, an elegant dressing-gown of velvet faced with cherry-colored silk, and velvet slippers.

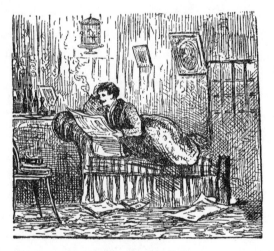

A Murderer's Cell

At ten o'clock on the morning of November 19, 1873 Maggie Jourdan appeared at the main entrance of the Tombs, which was then in Franklin Street, on her usual daily visit. She was given a pass and admitted without question. The lower part of her body was noticeably bulky, but the keepers assumed (or so they said later, though it was generally believed that they had been bribed) that she had simply put on additional petticoats to protect herself from the cold of a raw November day. She went immediately to Sharkey's cell, No. 40, on the second tier, and talked to him through the grating for several hours. The prison attachés had become so accustomed to seeing her about that they paid no attention to what she said and did. She was so well known, indeed, that often, though not on this particular day, she was permitted to enter the Tombs without a pass.

Mrs. Wesley Allen appeared at the prison about half past twelve o'clock and asked for a pass to visit a burglar named Flood, a friend of her husband's, who was confined in cell No. 95, on the third tier. She stopped at Sharkey's cell and greeted both the murderer and Maggie Jourdan, but after a few moments went on upstairs to the third tier, where she spent some time talking to Flood. At one o'clock Maggie Jourdan departed, an unusual circumstance, for she had never before been known to leave the prison until late in the afternoon. However, nothing was thought of it.

Half an hour later a peculiar-looking female, with unusually broad and powerful shoulders, walked calmly down the second-tier corridor, through the two lower gates, and out the main entrance, surrendering a pass to the keeper on guard. Passing into Franklin Street, she waited on the corner a few minutes and then boarded a Bleecker Street car. She wore a heavy black woolen dress, a black cloak, an Alpine bonnet, and a thick green barège veil which she kept pulled down close to her face. A patrolman, who saw her come out of the prison and was astonished at the nimbleness with which she boarded the trolley car, provided the additional information that she wore green stockings, and new gaiters, with high French heels.

At five minutes past two o'clock Mrs. Wesley Allen came

Sharkey's Escape

down the stairs and started to walk nonchalantly past the guard at the main entrance. He asked for her pass, and after she had fumbled in her dress and pockets for some time, she said:

"I put it in my pocket, but I must have lost it."

She was very nervous, and the guard called Warden Johnson, who detained her and ordered all the cells searched. In a few minutes it was discovered that Sharkey's cell was empty; he had escaped. His clothing, even his elegant dressing-gown and slippers, had been scattered about the cell; and on the shelf above the wash-basin were found the remnants of his flowing black mustache, which he had shaved. It was immediately obvious, even to the obtuse prison-keepers, that the peculiar-looking female had been Sharkey in disguise, that the dress which he had worn out of prison had been smuggled to him by Maggie Jourdan underneath her own garments, and that the pass which he had given up at the entrance had originally been issued to Mrs. Wesley Allen. The latter was immediately arrested, but nothing could be proved against her, and she was released when she continued to insist that she had lost the pass.

Maggie Jourdan was arrested that evening at the home of her mother, 167 Ninth Avenue. She greeted the detectives cheerfully and remarked that she was "the happiest little woman in the world." In due time she was tried before Recorder Hackett in General Sessions Court, and her chief counsel, the celebrated Big Bill Howe, defended her with such persuasive eloquence that the jury disagreed. She was promptly released and the indictment against her was quashed.

Nor was Sharkey ever recaptured, although the city offered a reward of two thousand dollars for him, dead or alive. He remained in New York for three weeks after his escape, protected by his political and underworld friends, and then shipped on a small schooner for Baracoa, Cuba. From there he went to Havana. The United States had no extradition treaty with Spain, and it was impossible to bring him back. Two years after he walked out of the Tombs, Maggie Jourdan joined him in Cuba, but in a few months Sharkey tired of her and cast her aside. She returned to the metropolis and dropped out of sight. Sharkey, so far as the police records show, never again appeared in New York.

THE ABOLITION RIOTS OF 1834

NEW YORK was never very friendly to the Abolition movement, and from the beginning of the anti-slavery agitation until the end of the Civil War there were frequent clashes between the Abolitionists and the pro-slavery element, which was mainly composed of the ruling Irish faction of Tammany Hall. Taking advantage of the great ovation accorded William Lloyd Garrison in London in 1833, the year in which slavery was declared illegal throughout the British Empire, the astute Tammany politicians succeeded in convincing the New York Irish that the Abolitionists, and Garrison in particular, were in reality British agents attempting to transform the Republic into a British colony. Consequently the feeling in the metropolis was as much anti-English and anti-Garrison as it was pro-slavery.

Throughout 1834 a fever of rioting pervaded New York. There were innumerable fights between rival fire companies and between the gangs of the Bowery and the Five Points, and three days of rioting marked the municipal elections in April, the first time a mayor of New York was elected by popular vote. Many of the minor brawls were stopped by High Constable Jacob Hays, who was famous for his skill in suppressing such disturbances single-handed. But even the redoubtable Hays was helpless before the mobs of from five hundred to a thousand men which roamed the streets during the election and Abolition troubles. Nor could he count on much assistance from the watchmen and the constables, who formed, respectively, the night and day police forces. Their combined strength seldom exceeded one hundred men. When serious riots occurred, it was nearly always necessary to mobilize the National Guard.

The Abolition disturbances began on July 7, 1834, when a mob attacked the Chatham Street (now Park Row) Chapel, where Negroes were holding religious services. Several of the latter were injured, and the interior of the church was wrecked. On the evening of July 9 a crowd of several hundred men, largely recruited from the Irish gangs of the Bowery and the Five Points, again gathered before the chapel and were harangued by the pro-slavery and Tammany spellbinders. Meanwhile Edwin Forrest was appearing at the Bowery Theater in a special performance of *Metamora* for the benefit of the stage manager, an Englishman named Farren, who had so often come under the disapproval of the Irish that the city authorities had advised him to leave the country. When the benefit was announced, anonymous placards appeared denouncing Farren as a British spy and asserting that he had spoken disrespectfully of the Americans. Some of these placards were distributed to the mob in front of the chapel, and it was soon surging up the Bowery. The doors of the theater were battered down with clubs and stones, and the rioters swept into the auditorium, yelling for Farren to come out and be hanged. Edwin Forrest advanced to the footlights and attempted to speak, but was soon howled down and withdrew. The mob then began to destroy seats and other furniture, throwing the audience into a panic, but before much damage was done, the rioters were clubbed from the theater by a strong detachment of watchmen.

But the larger crowd on the street would not disperse, and the excitement increased when several men obtained cowbells and began to ring them violently. Presently someone shouted that the hanging of an Abolitionist would be a fitting end to the night's pleasure, and a score suggested that the victim be Arthur Tappan, president of the American Anti-Slavery Society and a founder of the *Journal of Commerce*. The mob streamed wildly down the Bowery, but its leaders apparently changed their minds, and instead of going to Arthur Tappan's house the rioters stopped in front of the home of his brother Lewis, equally prominent in the Abolition movement, on Rose Street. Lewis Tappan and his family had been warned by a watchman who raced ahead of the mob, and had fled in their night-clothes to the home of a neighbor, where they hid in the cellar. Finding the house undefended, the rioters smashed the doors and windows and wrecked the interior. The furniture was piled in the street and set on fire. In taking down the pictures one of the brawlers found a portrait of George Washington, and when another tried to snatch it, he cried:

"It's Washington! For God's sake, don't burn Washington!"

His cry was heard in the street, and a great shout went up: "For God's sake, don't burn Washington!"

A score of hoodlums formed in line, and the picture of the first President was passed carefully into the street and solemnly escorted to the porch of a neighboring house. It was not damaged. Soon afterwards the mob met and defeated a small detail of watchmen, but dispersed when the fire-engines arrived.

At dusk the next day, July 10, a large crowd assembled before Lewis Tappan's home, and several men were preparing to fire the ruins when the watchmen charged. The rioters fell back and swept across the city to the Laight Street Presbyterian Church, of which the Reverend Dr. Samuel Cox, an active Abolitionist, was pastor. The doors and windows were soon smashed, but before the mob could enter the building, a strong force of watchmen appeared under the command of Mayor Cornelius W. Lawrence. The rioters fled as before, but re-formed a few blocks away and raced yelling to the home of Dr. Cox, on Charlton Street. They found the house empty and the doors barricaded, for during the afternoon Dr. Cox had removed his furniture and had left the city with his family. When the watchmen again appeared, the rioters crowded into Charlton Street, about a block from the Cox residence. There they erected a barricade of carts and furniture tied together, and armed themselves with fence pickets and paving blocks. Members of one of the Five Points gangs each took up two enormous paving stones and smote them together in unison, shouting: "All together!" They produced a terrific din, but made no effort to surmount their barricade and attack the watchmen. Nor did the latter move forward to the assault.

They remained facing the mob for several hours. At two o'clock in the morning the rioters dispersed, a few stragglers passing the church on Laight Street and breaking more windows.

On the afternoon of July 11 Mayor Lawrence issued a proclamation calling upon all good citizens to aid in maintaining order and asked Major-General Shadford to call out the National Guard. The Twenty-seventh Regiment of Infantry was immediately put under arms, and the various companies were assembled at City Hall, the Arsenal, and the City Bazaar. At dusk the streets were again thronged with marching men who poured out of the Bowery, the Five Points, and the waterfront dives of the Fourth Ward. Several hundred converged upon Arthur Tappan's silk-store, on Pearl Street, before which twenty watchmen had been stationed. The mob began to stone the building and attacked ferociously when the watchmen attempted to capture the ringleaders. Many policemen and city officials were wounded. One alderman was stabbed and frightfully beaten, but he courageously crawled to the steps of the store and shouted that the building was filled with armed men who would turn cannon and muskets upon the rioters if the door were battered down. The mob hesitated and was at length chased away by a large force of watchmen.

While Tappan's store was under fire, other mobs were operating in different parts of the city, doing great damage to residences and stores on Spring, Catherine, Thompson, Reade, and Laight Streets and in the area around the Five Points, where the largest crowd of all had gathered. The Five Points mob appeared to be well organized, for runners were kept passing between the leaders, and scouts patrolled the streets to give warning of the approach of the watchmen or the soldiers. But the troops were busy elsewhere, and the watchmen were afraid to venture into the haunts of the desperate Five Pointers. For several hours the rioters were not molested, and in that time they did much damage. A dozen houses, including St. Philip's Negro church on Centre Street, were sacked and set on fire, and by midnight a dense pall of smoke overlay all of lower New York. Five houses of prostitution were wrecked and the torch applied, and the inmates were shamefully mistreated. Several English sailors were captured and mutilated, as were half a dozen Negroes. The rioting continued until one o'clock in the morning, when the blare of bugles told of the coming of the military. The mob then scattered, and an hour later the Five Points was quiet.

Some three hundred men, most of whom were recognized as criminals and bullies from the Bowery and the Five Points, assembled before the Laight Street Church during the early evening of that same day, July 11, but made no overt move until about nine o'clock, when they were reinforced by another mob, which swarmed out of Varick Street, brandishing brickbats and paving stones. Without halting, the rioters charged the watchmen who had been stationed before the church. Outnumbered, the watchmen retreated, and the mob proceeded to smash every remaining window of the building. At Beach Street the police rallied, and a messenger was sent to City Hall. Mayor Lawrence immediately ordered the troops into action, and within half an hour the Twenty-seventh Regiment, with loaded muskets and pistols, was marching to the scene of the riot, followed by a small detachment of cavalry.

Meanwhile the mob had abandoned the Laight Street Church and had attacked another church, on Spring Street. The fence surrounding the edifice was destroyed, and the windows and doors broken. Surging into the church, the rioters tore down the pulpit, ripped away the pews, and chopped great holes in the floor. Then they barricaded the street with the church furniture and with carts chained and roped together. Before the soldiers appeared, three rows of barricades had been constructed, behind which the rioters crouched with their hands and arms laden with brickbats, stones, pitchforks, knives, and clubs. The regiment was almost up to war strength, and a thousand bayonets gleamed in the moonlight as the troops marched steadily forward. Colonel Stevens, in command, halted the soldiers near the first barricade, and while the front ranks leveled their muskets, the regiment's pioneers rushed forward with axes. The barricade was soon demolished, and, cowed by the threatening muskets, the rioters, who had thought to defend it, moved sullenly back to their second line of defense. There a similar method of assault was employed, and again the mob fell back, hurling a shower of bricks and stones as it retreated.

The third barricade was the most formidable of all, and behind it the rioters were massed in great numbers. City officials who had accompanied the regiment advised Colonel Stevens to fire a volley into the swarm, but the Colonel again ordered his pioneers to the front under cover of the infantrymen, and once more the rioters gave way. Then the soldiers, and the watchmen under command of Justice Olin D. Lowndes and High Constable Hays, pursued the rioters through the side streets, clubbing them unmercifully. Not a shot was fired. Most of the members of the mob rushed back to the Five Points and joined the rioters there, but a hundred or so turned aside and assailed the home of the Reverend Mr. Ludlow, on Thompson Street near Prince. The minister, his wife, and their children hid in the cellar while the rioters overran the house, smashing windows and furniture. The soldiers appeared, finally, and the mob rushed into the street and vanished in the direction of the Five Points.

The following morning, several other regiments of the National Guard were mustered into service, and Mayor Lawrence swore in several hundred citizens as special constables and watchmen. Accompanied by armed soldiers, the watchmen searched the city for the known leaders of the mobs and arrested one hundred and fifty men, most of whom were quickly released by Tammany politicians. Fewer than twenty were tried and convicted.

WHEN THE PUNISHMENT FITTED THE CRIME

THE WAY of the transgressor, now paved with radio programs, baseball games, moving pictures, and a large measure of self-government, was really hard when New York was a municipal infant. It was especially so during the early days of Sing Sing, where for many years all of New York's convicted felons were incarcerated. The famous prison on the Hudson opened in the late spring of 1828, with six hundred damp and dismal cells, each seven feet high, seven feet deep, and three and one-half feet wide. Each cell was occupied by from two to five men, although the original plan was to give each prisoner a compartment to himself. The convicts wore striped suits, marched in the lock-step, and were burdened with the ball and chain whenever they left their cells. They were allowed no recreation, and no exercise save what they could obtain working on the rock-pile or in the prison shops. Absolute silence was imposed except at infrequent intervals. The keepers carried cats-o'-nine-tails, with which the prisoners were whipped for the slightest infraction of the rules. The use of the lash as a correctional measure was prohibited by the legislature in 1847, but as late as sixty years ago the Sing Sing authorities enforced discipline with various appliances which were almost as terrible as the machines with which the Holy Inquisition changed the minds of heretics in an even more barbarous age. Chief among them were the Shower-bath, the Bishop's Mitre, the Wooden Horse, the Spanish Crib, the Yoke, and the Thumb-String.

The Showerbath was a cabinet in which the convict was held immovable by clamps about his neck, wrists, and ankles. Four or five feet above his head was a large tank, from which water poured through a sieve with holes about a quarter of an inch in diameter, and so close together that by the time water struck the victim, it had converged into a single stream of considerable force. The water gathered in a shallow trough about the convict's head, so that he was in danger of drowning unless he kept his chin tilted and received it upon his forehead. The flow was regulated by a valve and was sometimes reduced to a tiny trickle, which pelted the prisoner's head for hour after hour. One barrel of water was usually enough to subdue the most stubborn man, but it is on record that one convict, a Manhattan lawyer serving a sentence for blackmail, sustained the shock of three barrels before admitting a violation of the prison rules.

The Bishop's Mitre was an open framework of iron, shaped roughly like a pear. It was placed over the convict's head so

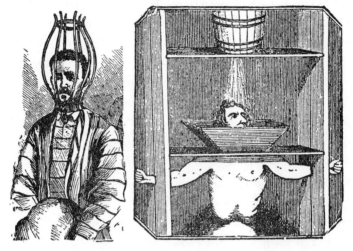

The Bishop's Mitre and the Showerbath

that it rested on his shoulders, and was locked in front with a padlock. The prisoner was compelled to wear it day and night, sometimes for weeks at a time. If a convict had been particularly refractory, that part of the framework which touched his shoulders was roughened and chipped, so that it bruised and scraped his flesh.

The Yoke resembled an ordinary horse's collar, but was constructed of iron and oak and had no padding whatever. It was also locked about a prisoner's neck, and jutted out about two feet front and back. A convict burdened with the Yoke was unable to lie down except with great difficulty; he was compelled to sleep sitting, or leaning awkwardly and painfully against a wall.

The Wooden Horse, called also the Spanish Donkey, was sometimes carved to resemble a real horse, but was more often the ordinary saw-horse on which the carpenter saws his boards and which is used as a table support at picnics and outings. The ridge was generally sharp. The convict bestrode the horse, and chains and chunks of iron were attached to his ankles, their weight depending upon the degree of pain and discomfort which the prison authorities wished to inflict. Occasionally short spikes were imbedded in the horse's back. Beside the unfortunate rider stood a keeper with a cat-o'-nine-tails, to discourage any idea of clambering down from the painful perch before the allotted time had expired. The Wooden Horse was also much used by the early Dutch as a method of punishing miscreants. It was introduced into the colony late in 1638, when two soldiers bestrode its sharp back for two hours. On the occasion the horse was stationary, but in later years it was usually mounted on a cart and hauled about the city, to the added pain and humiliation of the victim. The first woman to be so punished was one Mary Price. The old records do not divulge the nature of her crime, but they do say that her cries were heard from end to end of the city. Another who rode the Wooden Horse was Philip Geraerdy, a soldier, who in May 1642 occupied the perch for two hours, with a drawn sword in one hand and a pitcher of water in the other. A year or so later Geraerdy opened an inn on the present site of the Produce Exchange, which he called The Sign of the Wooden Horse. The authorities, however, considered that he was attempting to ridicule the processes of law and order, and he changed the name to The White Horse Tavern.

The Spanish Crib was probably the most inhuman machine ever used in an American prison. It was a large box with a movable floor, which was raised and lowered by means of pulleys and ropes. The convict was placed in the box, and his neck caught in a stock. Then the floor was slowly raised. This compelled him to bend his legs at the knees and to sus-

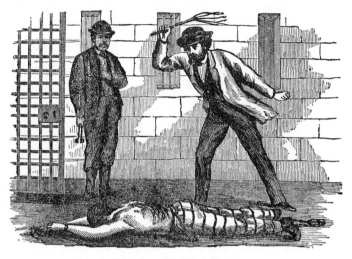

The Cat-O'-Nine-Tails

tain the entire weight of his body in that position. If he tried
to settle down, he was strangled by the clamps about his
throat. The Crib was very popular with the authorities of
Sing Sing for a year or two, but it was abandoned when it was
found that practically every man who experienced its horrors
was permanently crippled.

The Thumb-String was a modification of the Spanish
Crib. The convict was tied by the thumbs to the ceiling of the
box, and the floor was lowered beneath his feet. He was thus
left dangling by the thumbs. One minute of this torture was
about all that the strongest man could stand, and it was
resorted to only in extreme cases.

All of these appliances were almost constantly in use at
Sing Sing until as recently as the early eighteen-seventies,
when they were abolished by the legislature. After that the
worst punishment inflicted was solitary confinement. This
was considered very humane because there was little actual

physical pain. Few men, however, could undergo the terrors of solitary in the dark, mephitic cells of old Sing Sing without lasting damage to their mental and nervous systems. Many came out raving maniacs. Now, of course, even solitary confinement is forbidden except in rare instances. Generally a refractory convict is punished by the withholding of some of the many privileges which he enjoys.

The methods of punishment employed by the early Dutch, and also by the English who succeeded them as masters of the colony, were no more calculated to coddle the evil-doer than were those used in later years at Sing Sing. In Colonial times persons accused of crimes were commonly examined under torture, and those convicted of capital offenses were hanged, broken on the wheel, drawn and quartered, branded and gashed, burned at the stake, or expelled from the city. Sometimes they were chained hand and foot and hung up in cages at the Battery, to die of thirst and starvation.

The first attempt at capital punishment in New York was made in 1641. Nine Negroes, all owned by the Dutch West India Company, were tried for the murder of another Negro, and all pleaded guilty, thereby placing the judges in an awkward dilemma, for to hang so many servants of the company would have been extravagant. It was finally decided that the Negroes should draw lots to determine which should be "punished by the cord until death." The choice fell upon Manuel Gerritt, popularly known as Manuel the Giant, who is said to have been the biggest man on Manhattan Island. About the giant's throat the hangman strapped two strong halters, but both broke under his weight when the wagon on which he stood had been driven out from under him. They tried again with three halters, and when these also broke the assembled burghers clamored loudly for a pardon. This the Governor was pleased to grant, having discerned the hand of God in the matter.

The Pillory and the Stocks

As punishment for minor offenses the Dutch, and also the English for many years, used the ducking-stool, the pillory, the stocks, and the whipping-post, from the last of which the miscreant, having been whipped almost to the limit of his endurance, was hoisted into the air by straps buckled about his waist, and left there to dangle until it pleased his judges to take him down. Some of the punishments, as well as the offenses for which they were prescribed, sound a bit quaint to our modern ears. Humiliation was usually as much the object as the infliction of bodily pain. A farmer, having been convicted of slandering the Governor, was sentenced to stand at the gates of the Fort for twelve hours and at fifteen-minute intervals loudly beg that dignitary's pardon. A preacher was "scandalized by a female, who was forthwith summoned to appear and declare before the Council [the governing body of the colony] that she knew he was honest, and that she had lied falsely." Some time later the preacher's wife was accused of "having drawn up her petticoat a little way," but she was discharged with a reprimand. A ten-year-old girl was caught stealing, and it was ordered that "her mother chastise her with rods in the presence of the Worshipful Magistrates," although the Schout-Fiscal, an official who combined the duties of sheriff and district attorney, recommended solitary confinement on bread and water. A sailor who drew his knife on a comrade was sentenced to receive three lashes from each member of the crew of his ship and then to throw himself three times from the yard-arm. For the theft of a sack of corn a farm-hand was tied to a stake, gashed in the cheek, and banished from New York for twenty-five years. A Negro who had assaulted a constable was tied to the tail of a cart, which was driven about the city, preceded by a crier. At every street corner the cart stopped and the Negro received ten lashes on his bare back.

The Dutch incarcerated their prisoners in the gloomy dungeons of the Fort, south of Bowling Green, and in the Stadt Huys, on the site of Nos. 71 and 73 Pearl Street. The English used as a prison the basement of the new City Hall which they erected in 1700 at Wall and Broad Streets, on the present site of the Sub-Treasury. In 1756 the English built the first real jail in New York, a four-story stone structure in the present City Hall Park, then called variously the Fields and the Commons. In all of these institutions the prisoners were herded, a large number together, in large rooms, and quite often were chained to the floors and walls. The first State Prison was erected in 1796 in Greenwich Village, a fashionable settlement on the site of the old Indian town of Sappokanican. The buildings and grounds of the prison occupied four acres of land, and were enclosed by a stone wall fourteen feet high in front and twenty-three feet high in the rear. There were fifty-two cells, each of which was supposed to hold two men, but was generally occupied by four or five, and twenty-eight smaller compartments for solitary confinement.

The inmates of the Greenwich Village prison were employed, for the most part, in sewer and road-construction work and in filling cisterns and reservoirs for the use of the Fire Department. They wore brown jackets and trousers striped with white or gray, but if a man was a second offender the right side of his coat and the left side of his trousers were black. A third offender wore a large figure 3 on his back and received less food, and that of a coarser quality, than the others. The convicts worked twelve hours a day, during which time each man was laden with a heavy ball and chain. After the evening meal they were marched to their cells and locked in until next morning. Naturally enough, they developed a pronounced distaste for their surroundings, and attempts to escape were almost as numerous as in modern penal institutions. Outbreaks occurred at least once a year until 1828, when the prison was abandoned and the convicts transferred to Sing Sing. The Greenwich property was sold in 1829 and turned to commercial uses, part of the wall being built into a brewery.

BRISTOL BILL, THE BURGLAR

OF ALL the English criminals who found the United States a happy hunting-ground during the thirty years that preceded the Civil War, the most daring and probably the most successful was the second son of a member of the British Parliament from the city of Bristol, black sheep of an ancient and respectable family. Eventually he became known to the police of three continents as "Bristol Bill, the Burglar." In the eighteen-forties, he was frequently described in the New York newspapers and in the *Police Gazette* as "the most celebrated bank robber and burglar of our time." Moreover, he was a counterfeiter and a forger of extraordinary skill, and a swindler whose prosperous and gentlemanly appearance was calculated to inspire his victim with faith and assurance.

Among his criminal associates Bristol Bill was as famous for his devotion to the ladies as for the daring and resource with which he planned and executed his robberies. He never had fewer than three sweethearts, and for several years, from 1842 to 1849, he maintained three—one in Manhattan, another in Brooklyn, and a third in Jersey City. Curiously, his sweethearts were close friends.

When he traveled, they accompanied him, one posing as his wife and two as his sisters. When he was in trouble, they combined forces to provide him with alibis and other assistance. The bare mention of his name was enough to set hearts to fluttering among the felonious females; and with good reason, for he was considered the handsomest crook in America.

He was almost six feet tall, with keen black eyes, curly black hair, an elegantly trimmed beard and mustache, and an exceptionally broad forehead. His clothing was always extremely fashionable in cut, and of the best material. Because of his early training he found it easy to play the gentleman, although he did so only when he saw a chance for profit. Ordinarily his conduct was pretty low and his conversation coarse, laden with invective and billingsgate.

Throughout his American career Bristol Bill used, principally, the euphonious aliases of William Darlington and William H. Warburton. American detectives finally learned that he had been born at Bristol in 1802 and christened William, but his surname was probably never known in this country.

The London police knew it, but steadfastly refused to give the New York authorities any information about Bristol Bill's antecedents because of the prominence of his family. Such disclosure, they said, would be against the public interest. Not even the indefatigable George Wilkes, one of the founders of the *Police Gazette*, or the equally industrious James Gordon Bennett of the New York *Herald*, was able to solve the mystery of the noted burglar's identity, although they were chiefly instrumental in putting him in jail.

Bristol Bill himself refused to divulge the secret to George Thompson, a Boston journalist who in 1851, under the penname of "Greenhorn," wrote a highly moralistic work called *Bristol Bill, Being an Account of the Life and Exploits of This Notorious Burglar*. He did, however, give Thompson many details of his early life.

In 1823, when Bristol Bill was in his second year at Eton College, his father adopted the sixteen-year-old orphaned daughter of a poor curate. The member of Parliament had hoped that this praiseworthy action would bring joy and comfort into his home; instead, it provided the emotional fillip that turned his son's footsteps into criminal paths. Bill and the curate's child promptly fell in love and, as Bill's biographer puts it, "on the occasion of a somewhat lengthy visit at home, an unholy passion seized on the heart of the rash and unthinking youth, and in a moment of tempestuous love and tearful frenzy, the pleading voice and earnest expostulations of the fair being he adored were hushed, and her ruin was accomplished."

Discovery of their sin inevitably followed, and in a burst of maniacal rage the father knocked his son down and forthwith turned the erring maid from his door. Bill's mother received the news in a manner characteristic of early nineteenth-century femininity. She "retired to the solitude of her chamber, there to dwell in tears and prayer on the mournful evidence of wickedness which had caused her beloved adopted daughter to fall from the high estate of virtue, through the evil persuasion and mad passion of her own fond son."

Bill was ordered to return to his studies at Eton, but manfully refused to desert his sweetheart. He fled with her to London, thoughtfully taking with him seventy pounds which he had found in his father's escritoire. Soon after the birth of his child he obtained employment in the shop of a London locksmith, but quickly learned that the worthy smith was principally engaged in the manufacture of duplicate keys and burglar tools for a criminal gang called the Blue Boys. Bristol Bill promptly joined this aggregation of thieves and thereafter never drew an honest breath.

He operated successfully for half a dozen years most of that time as captain of the gang, but the police finally got so close upon the trail that the Blue Boys divided their plunder and scattered. According to his own estimate, Bill's share was approximately two hundred thousand dollars. He abandoned the curate's daughter and fled to Liverpool, hoping to take ship to America, but was arrested, and his loot confiscated, by a London policeman. Under vastly different circumstances this policeman and Bristol Bill were destined to meet again in New York.

After serving ten years of a fourteen-year sentence at Botany Bay, the British penal settlement in Australia, Bristol Bill escaped by swimming four miles to an American whaler. Eventually, he was put ashore at New Bedford, Massachusetts, and early in 1841 made his first appearance in New York. American criminal circles at this time were completely dominated by professional thieves and cracksmen from London and by escaped convicts and ticket-of-leave men from Australia. The argot of the English crook was the common slang of the day. The underworld generally was known as "the cross," and a criminal was called a "crossman" or was said to be "on the cross." These designations probably arose because in old England highwaymen customarily waited for their victims at cross-roads.

The most important gang then operating in New York, called by Bristol Bill's biographer "the most extensive association of burglars, counterfeiters, and swindlers that the Western world has ever seen," comprised such noted London crossmen as Billy Fish, Billy Hoppy, "Cupid" Downer, Bill Parkinson, Bob Whelan, Jim Honeyman, and Dick Collard. The only native Americans were Joe Ashley and "One-eye" Thompson, who in later years became a newspaper editor.

There was no titular leader, but the brains of the gang was Samuel Drury, who lived in a mansion in Astoria, Long Island, and owned a private bank at Canandaigua, in up-state New York. Drury was widely known in the metropolis as a capitalist and financier and ostensibly was a man of many important affairs. In reality he was, primarily, a manufacturer of counterfeit money, much of which he put into circulation through his own bank. He was also a "fence," or receiver of stolen goods. He handled everything stolen by members of the gang and kept the bulk of the profit for himself. He was a rich man.

Bristol Bill's first sweetheart in New York was a young girl named Catherine Davenport, who lived with him for several years and had two children by him. Besides being an expert sneak-thief and pick-pocket on her own account, she was employed by Drury as a "koneyacker," or passer of counterfeit money. She told her associates that Bristol Bill was in New York, and he was immediately invited to join the gang. They were all familiar with his reputation as captain of the Blue

Boys in London, and Hoppy, Fish, and Downer had also known him at Botany Bay, from which they had likewise escaped. Bristol Bill called upon Drury in Astoria, and after they had talked for some time, he suddenly asked:

"Drury, weren't you a London policeman ten or twelve years ago?"

"Yes," Drury admitted.

"I knew it!" exclaimed Bristol Bill. "You're the same hound that tracked me to Liverpool and had me pinched for fourteen years!"

"I remember you," said Drury. "I had to leave England myself soon afterwards, because I halved swag with a crossman. If you have any grudge against me, you must forget it. I can make your fortune in this country."

Bristol Bill finally consented to forgo the revenge of which he had dreamed, and worked hand-in-glove with Drury for several years. During this period he maintained headquarters in New York, but his criminal activities ranged along the Atlantic seaboard from New Orleans to Montreal, where he stole a large quantity of silver plate from the home of the Governor-General of Canada.

Eventually, however, at the behest of the *Police Gazette*, and after Drury had served his purpose as a fence, Bristol Bill obtained his revenge, trapping Drury into admissions that caused his arrest and started the breaking up of the gang. This was in 1849, when an infernal machine containing three pounds of giant powder was exploded in the home of Thomas Warner, a New York lawyer with whom Drury had quarreled.

Drury and One-eyed Thompson, together with Drury's son, were lodged in jail on the evidence procured by Bristol Bill and were also charged with counterfeiting when a search of Drury's mansion in Astoria disclosed plates and spurious notes. Other criminals were soon implicated, and within a year the gang had been crushed and half a dozen of its leading lights were in prison.

Bristol Bill was not suspected; nor, in fact, was he ever arrested for burglary either in New York or in Boston, the two cities in which he committed his most important crimes. In Boston, indeed, he was on such friendly terms with the authorities that the *Police Gazette* commonly referred to him as "the assistant chief of the Boston police." According to New York detectives, Bill's accomplices in Boston included a well-known broker and the cashier of a large bank.

Bristol Bill

For those days Bristol Bill's takings were enormous. In ten years of felonious enterprise in this country his income amounted to about four hundred thousand dollars, practically all of which he spent on women, fine clothing, and high living. When the prison doors finally clanged behind him, in his forty-eighth year, he had less than five dollars. His success was due to his daring, to the thoroughness with which he planned his crimes, to the fact that he invariably disposed of his loot as quickly as possible, and, last but not least, to his mechanical ingenuity.

He manufactured all of his own burglar tools, which the New York police said were the finest they had ever seen, and is said to have been the first man to use a curved jimmy, or a small crowbar. This tool, as developed by Bristol Bill, was very similar to the modern pinch bar commonly used by carpenters. He was also the first burglar to make a really practicable pair of nippers, thin pliers with which he reached into a lock to turn the key.

These implements are still used by criminals, although the sort of lock against which nippers would be effective is seldom found now except on interior doors. As a picker of locks and a fashioner of false keys Bristol was probably without an equal in the United States. He once escaped from a lock-up with a key made from a sliver of oak, and on another occasion succeeded in opening his cell door with a key which he had constructed from a strip cut from the stovepipe. This time, however, he was caught before he could scale the prison walls.

Bristol Bill's masterpiece of crime in this country was probably the robbery of the barge *Clinton*, which ran regularly during the summer months between New York and Poughkeepsie and daily conveyed large sums of money consigned to banks in both cities. Assisted by Honeyman, Parkinson, Collard, and Cupid Downer, Bristol Bill began planning the burglary early in March 1845, while the barge was being overhauled in the slip at Murray Street. He learned that the packages of money sent to Poughkeepsie banks were locked in an iron chest in the barge office.

The key to the chest was kept in the money-drawer of the

captain's chest. On the first trip of the barge in April 1845, Bristol Bill was a passenger, and, before he returned to New York, succeeded in obtaining a wax impression of the lock of the office door. From this he made a key.

He now began to follow the barge master, Captain Wiltsie, about the city, to make sure that he chose a day on which a large sum of money was being transferred. On April 7, 1845 he trailed Captain Wiltsie into the Phœnix Bank and saw him receive six large packages of bank-notes. At the Merchants' Exchange he received two more. Carrying the money wrapped in a large handkerchief, Captain Wiltsie returned to the barge and, as was his custom, deposited it in the iron chest.

Parkinson remained on the vessel as a look-out, while Bristol Bill hurried away to a side street, where Downer, Honeyman, and Collard waited with three wagons loaded with crates and barrels. They were driven at once to the barge for shipment to Poughkeepsie. Their arrival just before sailing-time created much commotion. All hands turned out to stow the unexpected freight, and Captain Wiltsie himself supervised the work; leaving his clerk alone in the office.

One of Bill's sweethearts, sailing as a passenger, now called the clerk from the office to complain about her accommodations. Bill immediately opened the door with his false key, jimmied the captain's desk, and found the key to the iron chest. A few moments later he sauntered off the barge with the money underneath his coat.

The loot amounted to thirty-two thousand dollars, in easily identified bank-notes of large denominations. Bristol Bill retained ten thousand dollars as his share, but immediately sold his notes to Sam Drury for seven thousand dollars. Drury put them out gradually through his own bank. Parkinson, Honeyman, Downer, and Collard foolishly tried to pass their own bills and were arrested almost immediately. Within a year they were in Sing Sing prison. The police suspected that Bristol Bill had planned the crime, but could find no evidence to justify his arrest, and his accomplices refused to betray him.

During the excitement of the smashing of Drury and his associates Bristol Bill was not molested by the police. Nevertheless, there was great potential danger for him in New York. He decided to seek new fields of labor. Accompanied by his current sweetheart, a former opera-singer known in the underworld as "Gookin Peg," by a counterfeiter named Christian Meadows, and by a London burglar called "English Jim," he went to Vermont and leased a cottage at Groton, near the Canadian border. The star of the famous burglar, however, was rapidly setting.

Acting on information furnished by the New York *Herald* and the *Police Gazette*, which had only hired him to expose Drury and bore him no allegiance, the Vermont authorities made a sudden search of the cottage in the spring of 1850. They found burglar tools, counterfeiting apparatus, and newly made bank-notes, besides diagrams of several banks which Bristol Bill had planned to rob. English Jim was away at the time and so escaped, and Gookin Peg was not arrested. Bill and Christian Meadows, however, were locked up in the county jail, together with two local crooks, who promptly turned state's evidence.

This raid ended Bristol Bill's career as a burglar. He was quickly convicted of possessing burglar tools, of counterfeiting, and of conspiring to rob five Vermont banks. He was sent to the state prison at Windsor for ten years and so passed from the American criminal scene. When his sentence expired, he was almost sixty years old, and, so far as the police knew, he never returned to New York. He is believed to have gone to England.

In any event, he dropped out of sight. Throughout his long imprisonment he never expressed the slightest remorse. On the contrary, he said that, so far as he knew, he had never made but one mistake. During his early days in London he invented an unpickable lock. This excellent article, which was widely sold in America and made its appearance several times on bank and house doors, caused Bristol Bill much annoyance.

THE FLOUR RIOT
OF 1837

THE INSTABILITY of the American financial and business
structure during the year that preceded the panic of 1837
added immeasurably to the distress that had been caused by
the great fire of 1835, in which nearly seven hundred buildings were destroyed, with a total loss of some twenty million
dollars. Few of the insurance companies were able to meet
their obligations after the fire, and financial houses and banks
were compelled to suspend operations, so that owners of factories and other business establishments were unable to
obtain money with which to rebuild. Consequently the thousands who had been thrown out of work by the ravages of the
flames remained idle during the following year. In the spring

of 1836 the alarm over the situation was increased by depressing reports from Virginia and other wheat-producing states, and by late summer it was apparent that the winter would see a decided scarcity of flour and a sharp advance in price. The great grain fields of the West were then a wilderness, and the bulk of America's wheat was grown east of the Allegheny Mountains. Some, of course, was imported from England and the Black Sea countries, but they also reported short crops.

By the early part of September 1836, flour was selling at seven dollars a barrel, and within a month had advanced to twelve dollars, with the demand far exceeding the visible supply. Commission merchants predicted that before the winter of 1836–37 was over, flour would go to the unheard-of price of twenty dollars a barrel. Bread soon became a scarce article of diet among the poor, and in the slums of the Five Points and the East Side thousands faced actual starvation. Their sufferings were increased by corresponding advances in the prices of other foodstuffs and of fuel, meat almost doubling and coal going to ten dollars a ton, although there was more coal on the market than there had been the previous year.

About February 1, 1837, reports were circulated that New York had but four weeks' supply of flour on hand, that there was no more in sight, and that the great flour and grain depot at Troy contained only four thousand barrels instead of the customary thirty thousand. The newspapers published these rumors under their largest headlines, and in inflammatory editorial articles denounced certain merchants who were said to be hoarding grain and flour, waiting for the inevitable advance in price. Great unrest prevailed throughout the city, and the Tammany heelers and politicians made political capital out of the situation by industriously spreading reports that England had refused to send flour to the United States, hoping thereby to starve the Irish who had become citizens of this country. The temperance agitators added fuel to the flames by asserting that the shortage of grain was due to the enormous quantities used by the breweries and distilleries.

During the first week in February a meeting was held in the Broadway Tabernacle, at which speeches were made and resolutions adopted, but all of them had a decided political complexion, and nothing practicable was proposed. Popular feeling now began to be directed against the merchants who had been accused of hoarding, and particularly against Eli Hart & Company in Washington Street between Dey and Cortlandt, and S. H. Herrick & Company, near Coenties Slip. The warehouses of both these companies were known to be packed with both wheat and flour and were protected by massive iron doors guarded by armed men. Rumors were afloat that these two firms alone had stored sufficient flour to tide the city over the emergency, and soon anonymous letters began to reach Hart, the Mayor, and High Constable Jacob Hays, warning them that unless the flour was released for consumption at a reasonable price the poor people would destroy Hart's store and seize the provisions. Hart only laughed at the warnings and refused to take additional precautions. Nor would he put any of his stock on the market.

The first direct action was taken on the morning of February 10, when the following placard appeared on the streets:

BREAD! MEAT!
RENT! FUEL!

The Voice of the People Shall be Heard and Will Prevail!

The People will meet in the Park [City Hall Park], rain or shine, at four o'clock on

MONDAY AFTERNOON

To inquire into the cause of the present unexampled distress, and to devise a suitable remedy. All friends of humanity, determined to resist monopolies and extortioners, are invited to attend.

The call was signed by Moses Jacques, Paulus Hedle, Daniel A. Robertson, Warden Hayward, Daniel Graham, John Windt, Elijah F. Crane, and Alexander Ming, Jr., who had several times been a candidate for city registrar. Moses Jacques acted as chairman when the crowd assembled, and by dusk between four and five thousand dirty and ragged men, most of them hailing from the rookeries of the Bowery and the Five Points, were surging about the speakers' stand. Alexander Ming made the first speech, but he became so excited that he wandered from his subject and launched into a harangue in which he attributed all the troubles of the Republic to the issue of banknotes. He urged his hearers, most of whom had not owned so much as a penny for weeks, to refuse banknotes and accept nothing but specie, whereat they howled in glee and voted wildly in favor of a resolution embodying that principle, which Ming offered for their approval. Then the men nearest him lifted him to their shoulders and carried him across the Park to Tammany Hall, then at Nassau and Frankfort Streets, where he took them into the bar and bought whisky for all hands.

Others whose names appeared upon the placard made very inflammatory speeches, however, blaming various agencies, from England to Eli Hart and S. H. Herrick, for the shortage of wheat and flour. They depicted Hart and other rich men as wallowing in luxury while the poor had no bread or fuel, and one of them concluded his harangue with "Fellow-citizens, Mr. Eli Hart has fifty-three thousand barrels of flour in his store. Let us go there and offer eight dollars a barrel for it, and if he will not take it . . ." He closed on this note of suggested violence, though he asserted afterwards that he had added: "we shall depart in peace." Every man within hearing of his voice promptly surged out of the Park and started down Broadway toward the store of Eli Hart & Company, followed by the remainder of the mob. They streamed through Cortlandt Street into Washington, and Hart's watchmen, hearing their shouts and curses, hurriedly closed the great iron doors and retreated into the store.

But in their haste they neglected to bar the center door, and it soon gave way to the battering assault of the rioters. A great throng swarmed into the building and scattered through the various floors and rooms. Eli Hart, who had been standing a block away watching his property, ran to City Hall and asked for a guard of watchmen. Twenty men were sent, but when they marched down Dey Street, the mob attacked them and took away their clubs. Nevertheless, they managed to make their way into the store and, with sticks provided by Hart, chased away those of the crowd who had gained entrance. By this time the Mayor had arrived, and he mounted the steps of the store and began to harangue the mob, but he was assailed with such a shower of bricks and stones that he was compelled to retire.

The rioters then made a rush for the doors, and wrenching one of them from its hinges, employed it as a battering ram, soon demolishing the others. Through the three doorways the mob poured, routing the watchmen and clerks. One gang invaded Hart's private office and destroyed his documents and furniture and stole a considerable sum of money. Other groups climbed the stairway to the storerooms and, after breaking the windows, began rolling barrels of flour and sacks of wheat to the sills and dumping them into the street. Most of the kegs were staved in when they struck the pavement, and the others were soon smashed by the rioters, who had set up a singsong chant of "Here goes flour at eight dollars a barrel!" Within a few moments the street was ankle-deep in flour and wheat, and men were filling their hats and pockets, while women who had been attracted by the disturbance were gathering up large quantities of flour in their aprons and skirts. The mob had destroyed five hundred barrels of flour and a thousand bushels of wheat in sacks when a large body of watchmen appeared, supported by two companies of the Twenty-seventh Regiment of the National Guard. Frightened by the clubs of the watchmen and the glistening bayonets of the soldiers, the mob fled, but some fifty of the ringleaders were captured and placed under arrest. A detail of police commanded by Watchman Bowyer started with them to the jail, but they had gone no more than two blocks when rioters attacked them and rescued the prisoners.

Meanwhile the bulk of the mob, routed by the watchmen and the troops, had rushed across the city and attacked Herrick & Company's warehouse, smashing the doors and windows with paving stones and brickbats. The rioters began rolling out barrels of flour and sacks of wheat and within ten minutes had destroyed thirty barrels and about a hundred bushels of grain. Then, for some unknown reason, the throng of men and women suddenly fled from the store, and the rioting was over. Some of the rioters said afterwards that they left the Herrick store because the owner had promised to give all his flour to the poor, but Mr. Herrick vehemently denied this. Moreover, he didn't do it. The next day the price of flour increased one dollar a barrel.

CHAPTER 20

SPORTSMAN'S PARADISE

DURING THE early days of Dutch and English rule, and for nearly fifty years after the establishment of the American Republic, the present site of New York City was a veritable paradise for the hunter and the fisherman. Game of almost every description, including deer, bear, and occasionally bison and panther, roamed Manhattan Island from Spuyten Duyvil to the Battery and throughout the remainder of the area now included in the Greater City; the harbor fairly teemed with sharks, whales, and porpoises, which often ran up the East and Hudson Rivers and were captured; and fish in innumerable variety abounded in the coastal waters of Manhattan and in the numerous inland streams and ponds.

Some of the fish which succumbed to the prowess of the Dutch and English anglers were enormous. Sturgeon ten and twelve feet long, and salmon measuring six feet from nose to tail, were frequently taken from the Hudson, while from the waters of the harbor and the East and Harlem Rivers fishermen brought to market lobsters five and six feet long, crabs as large as dinner plates, shrimp from ten inches to a foot in length, and oysters so huge that three or four sufficed for a family of five. For many years after the Dutch had settled Manhattan Island, the finest oyster beds in the East were between the Battery and Ellis Island, which was originally called Oyster Island.

The fish were as numerous as they were gigantic. As late as 1756 a Gravesend fisherman caught 7,500 shad at one haul of a seine off the Brooklyn shore, and catches of 4,000 to 5,000 at one cast were not uncommon. In 1813 a catch of 72,000 mackerel at one haul was reported. These fish were so plentiful around New York that year that they sold for a shilling a dozen, regardless of size. The shad was the first of the important food fish to appear in Manhattan and Brooklyn waters in the spring of the year, and the first one caught each season was presented with considerable ceremony to the Governor. He usually had it planked, a method of cookery which the Dutch had learned from the Indians. The fish was split and fastened to a piece of birch bark, cooked before the embers of a wood fire, and served on a bark platter with suitable embellishments. Neither the Dutch, nor the English who succeeded them as masters of the colony, would eat the roe, but the Indians cured the eggs both of the shad and of the sturgeon and put them away as winter provisions, considering them great delicacies. There was extraordinarily fine fishing in both the East and the Hudson Rivers, and in the Harlem River, which separates Manhattan from the mainland, until about the middle of the last century, when the city began emptying sewers into the streams. One of the great angling-places of those days was a bridge which connected the Battery and Castle Garden, now the site of the Aquarium. With hand lines fishermen caught great quantities of weakfish, striped bass, drums, and fish of other varieties. In later years the bridge was torn down and the cove filled in. A similar abundance of fish was to be found in the freshwater streams. In 1828, in a pond on the outskirts of Brooklyn, two men caught 111 trout, one of which weighed more than ten pounds. What these two gamehogs did with them is not recorded.

Salmon are unheard-of in New York waters now, but they were so plentiful during the first hundred years of the city's existence that servants signing bonds to work for a specified term of years stipulated that they were not to be required to eat salmon more than twice a week. Attempts were made to restock the Hudson with salmon some forty or fifty years ago, but they failed because of the polluted condition of the water and the destruction of the natural food with which the river formerly abounded. Sturgeon were extraordinarily plentiful in the Hudson, especially around Albany, where for many years they were known as "Albany beef." They seldom sold for more than a few cents a pound and were a staple food of the poor. The roe was seldom used, even a hundred years ago.

The sturgeon is an extremely powerful fish and in pursuit of its prey makes great leaps from the water. The enormous ones with which the Hudson swarmed were a source of considerable danger to fishermen and others whose business took them upon the water, as they often plunged through the bottoms of small boats. Once when an old Dutch woman was rowing across the Hudson in a batteau, a shallow, flat-bottomed boat tapering toward the ends, a great sturgeon broke water, flung itself into the boat, and crashed through the bottom planking. With great presence of mind the old woman sat on the hole, filling it so full of herself and her innumerable petticoats (no Dutch vrouw ever wore fewer than eight or ten such garments, all of heavy wool) that she stopped the leak and was towed safely to shore by another boat which had put out to her rescue.

Historians of early New York frequently mention the killing of whales along the Manhattan and Brooklyn shores, and for more than a century the whaling industry was a thriving business all along Long Island. In 1766 six men and two boys who were out fishing in a row-boat saw a forty-nine-foot whale run ashore on Coney Island, now a part of Brooklyn, and killed it with a rusty sword. "In the month of March, 1647," wrote the Dutch historian Van der Donck, "two whales, of common size, swam up the [Hudson] river forty miles, from which place one of them returned and stranded about twelve miles from the sea, near which place four others stranded the same year. The other ran up the river and stranded near the great Cahoos Falls, about forty-three miles from the sea. This fish was tolerably fat, for although the citizens of Rensselaerwyck boiled out a great quantity of train oil, still the whole river was oily for three weeks, and covered with grease."

As late as 1825 half a dozen men still followed the profession of catching sharks off the Manhattan docks and slips, particularly those near the fish markets. Probably the most successful of them was an old man known as Sam Way, who for several years around 1815 caught sharks off the slip at Catharine Market. He often caught as many as seven in one day, some as long as fourteen feet.

During the early days of the American metropolis deer and wild turkey were so plentiful in the forests of Manhattan Island that they often came down to the settlements to feed around the barn-yards. They were so easily captured, and so cheap, that a knife or a tobacco-pouch was considered a fair price for the dressed carcass of a deer. These animals had become such a pest on Manhattan by 1650 that the settlers hired Indians and small boys, armed with sticks, to stand guard over their fields and gardens and drive the animals away from the growing grain and vegetables. Bears were also numerous on Manhattan Island and in the territory that now forms the borough of Brooklyn, but were seldom eaten except by the Indians and Negro slaves. In 1679 a fine fat bear was shot in an orchard about where Maiden Lane and Broadway now intersect. Wild turkeys, weighing from twenty to forty pounds, roamed the island in innumerable flocks, thirty to fifty birds in a flock. They were shot from their roosting-places in the trees at night, caught by dogs in the snow, or taken with snares and were so common in the markets that a twenty-pound turkey was worth less than fifteen cents. There were so many ducks, geese, brant, swans, and other waterfowl that people living near the sea and along the shores of the streams and lakes complained of the noise made by the birds, and annually petitioned the authorities to destroy them. On several occasions when the birds annoyed high officials, companies of soldiers were sent out to exterminate as many as possible, which they did with blunderbusses loaded with nails and scrap iron. The historian Van der Donck wrote about the middle of the seventeenth century that swans were so numerous along Manhattan "that the bays and shores which they resort appear as if dressed in white drapery." A Dutch gunner in 1650 killed eleven gray geese at one shot from a stand near the present site of the Customs House, and another, shooting from cover at the Battery, brought down twenty-five wild ducks with a single blast from an old blunderbuss.

One of the great spectacles of the year in old New York was the semi-annual flight of wild pigeons. These birds appeared in flocks of such size as to obscure the sun for several hours, as if a thick cloud had passed before it. The beating of the millions of wings made a noise comparable to that of a squadron of aeroplanes. They flew low, and thousands were slaughtered each year by men who stood in the cleared spaces of the line of flight and swept long poles back and forth. A gun fired into the mass invariably killed from fifty to a hundred birds. One of their breeding-places was Big Pigeon Mountain, about forty miles northwest of Saratoga Springs, where they gathered in such vast numbers as to break the boughs of the pines and other trees in which they roosted. Wild pigeons were still plentiful in New York, although of course not on Manhattan Island, as late as seventy-five years ago, but they were never protected, and countless thousands were killed by game-hogs during the nesting-season. Now they are probably extinct; at any rate, none has been reported for at least ten years in the Catskill and Adirondack Mountains, where they were once so numerous.

HANDSOME JIM GULICK

THE MOST popular man who ever headed the New York Fire Department was probably James Gulick, better known as "Handsome Jim," who stood six feet and two inches in his socks, possessed tremendous physical strength, and is said to have been the finest-looking fireman in the New York of his day. Gulick, for many years a member of Engine Company 11, was appointed an assistant engineer in 1824, and in 1831 became chief engineer.

He led the firemen in the great fire of 1835, and after the flames had been extinguished, the newspapers and many prominent citizens praised his conduct, but several politicians whom he had prevented from meddling with the affairs of the department criticised him severely and at length induced the Common Council to order an investigation. The Fire and Water Committee of the Council held a special meeting on May 3, 1836 at which Alderman Paul, of the 4th Ward, bitterly denounced the chief engineer and demanded his removal from office. Gulick promptly gave the Alderman the lie, and departed, whereupon the committee went into secret session and voted unanimously to recommend his dismissal to the Common Council. This action, however, was not made public.

Next afternoon, a few hours before the scheduled meeting of the Common Council, fire was discovered in the Union Market at Houston and Second Streets. Because of the importance of the district, most of the fire companies answered the alarm, and Gulick took charge of the work of fighting the flames. The fire was well under control when Charles G. Hubbs, of Engine Company 13, who had learned what had happened at the session of the committee, approached Gulick and said:

"Boss, your throat is cut!"

"It can't be possible!" protested Gulick.

"It is," Hubbs persisted. "The committee has recommended your removal."

Gulick stepped back a few paces, reversed his hat, which he had been wearing with the broad black apron to the front to protect his face from the heat, and walked solemnly down the line of fire-engines and hose-carts. The gravity of his demeanor attracted the attention of the firemen, several of whom asked what had occurred.

"I am your chief no longer," Gulick replied. "They have voted to remove me."

The news spread quickly, and when it had been confirmed,

the firemen stopped working their engines and hauled the apparatus back to their company houses. The fire promptly started afresh, and another alarm was rung. The firemen answered it, but arrived with their hats reversed in imitation of Gulick's gesture, and declared that they would not work until Gulick had been reinstated.

James Gulick

A messenger was hurriedly dispatched to City Hall to apprise Mayor Cornelius W. Lawrence of the situation, and the Mayor forthwith hastened to the scene, bearing his staff of office and other emblems of authority. He commanded the firemen to throw water on the flames, and attempted to direct them, but they hooted at him and cheered lustily for the chief engineer. They finally became so threatening that the Mayor was compelled to retreat. He returned to City Hall and, finding the Common Council in session, angrily demanded that Gulick be dismissed at once, which was done. John Ryker, Jr., an assistant engineer, was appointed to succeed him.

By this time the fire had assumed serious proportions, and it was apparent that unless something was done, several blocks, and perhaps all that part of the city, would be destroyed. Carlisle Norwood, a fire warden, induced John Coger, foreman of Engine Company 8, to put his men to work, but they had no sooner manned the brakes than other firemen cut the hose in half a dozen places.

Norwood and another fire warden, Benjamin H. Guion, then went in search of Gulick and found him at his office in Canal Street, where he operated a small crockery business. After a great deal of discussion Gulick at length agreed to return to the fire, and a few minutes later he walked down the line of engines shouting:

"Now, boys, let's put this fire out. We will attend to the Fire and Water Committee afterwards."

Cheering madly, the firemen set to work and within a short time had extinguished the flames.

Indignation meetings were held next day in every firehouse in the city, and the firemen adopted resolutions notifying the city authorities that they would abandon their apparatus unless Gulick was restored to office. They repeated their demands several times during the ensuing week, but at length, finding that the Common Council paid no attention to them, eight hundred firemen marched in a body to City Hall and presented their resignations.

The men who had left their posts organized the "Resigned Firemen's Association" and swore eternal fealty to Gulick. They nominated the former chief engineer for city registrar that autumn, and when Tammany Hall refused him a place on the Democratic ticket, they procured an indorsement from the Whigs, who had always been in the minority in New York and were anxious to obtain support. After a strenuous and bitter campaign Gulick defeated the Tammany candidate by 6,054 votes, the largest majority ever received by an office-seeker in New York up to that time. At the spring elections the following year the firemen again voted solidly against Tammany Hall, and the Whigs gained control of the city for the first time. Every Whig candidate had been pledged to remove Ryker, and he was dismissed from office at the first session of the new Common Council. Cornelius V. Anderson, a member of Engine Company 1, was appointed chief engineer, and all of the resigned firemen immediately returned to their companies. The Whig Council also passed an ordinance authorizing the board of foremen and assistant foremen to elect the chief engineer thereafter.

However, Tammany was not yet through with the Gulick faction. In 1839 the astute Tammany politicians defeated the Whigs, and as soon as they had organized their Common Council, twenty prominent Democratic politicians formed twenty hose companies, which were reported to the Council at a secret midnight meeting of which only Tammany aldermen and assistant aldermen had been notified. The only Whig present was David Graham, assistant alderman from the 15th Ward, who had heard that the Council intended to induct the new organizations into the Fire Department, and had determined to prevent it if possible. He protested against the proposed action, and when his objections were ignored, he rose in his seat and solemnly proclaimed:

"At this dead hour of the night you are going to do the darkest deed ever perpetrated by human beings!"

He stalked from the chamber, and the Council, unabashed, proceeded to legalize the new companies. This added twenty foremen and a like number of assistant foremen to the board of foremen and assistants, which nominated the chief engi-

neer, and gave Tammany Hall control of that body. A meeting was immediately held, and the Tammany candidate for
chief engineer, Edward M. Hoffmire, of Engine Company 6,
was elected over Anderson by nine votes.

But the action of the Common Council had precipitated
a terrific uproar; the firemen angrily threatened dire political vengeance, and the newspapers published denunciatory
editorials pointing out that the new companies had no equipment, and that none of their members had ever had any fire-
fighting experience. They were sneeringly referred to as
political firemen, but were more generally known as "June
Bugs" because they had been appointed during the month of
June. In the records of the time the troubles are always
referred to as the June Bug excitement. Reporters were
unable to find more than a dozen of the new men who had
any idea what sort of apparatus they were supposed to operate, and Oliver Charlick, a Tammany politician, set the whole
town laughing by announcing: "I belong to one of those
things that spins around in the middle [meaning a hose-reel],
but I've never been able to find out where she lays."

The outburst of criticism finally frightened even Tammany
Hall, and the Common Council neglected to confirm
Hoffmire's election. Anderson therefore remained chief
engineer until he was succeeded by Alfred Carson in 1848 and
retired to become head of the Insurance Patrol. Fewer than
half a dozen of the new companies ever effected a permanent
organization, most of them dropping out of the department
as soon as they had accomplished their purpose.

Gulick was again a candidate for Registrar, but was
defeated and sank into the obscurity of private life. He eventually failed in business and died in want.

"WHERE IS THY STING?"

IMPORTANT AND picturesque functionaries of New York during the early days of Dutch and English rule were the Comforters of the Sick and the Inviters to Funerals, first appointed and licensed by the Common Council in 1690. There were two Comforters and two Inviters. They wore identical uniforms—tall black hats, solid black coats, and black mantles—and each carried a Bible and a long staff. When a man fell ill, the Comforters, their fees having been guaranteed by the patient's family or other relatives, sat at his bedside during the long hours of the night, reading the more lugubrious portions of the Scriptures, singing hymns, and otherwise preparing him for a possible journey to Kingdom Come.

When the patient died, as was not unusual despite these ministrations, the Comforters retired and the Inviters to Funerals took charge. Attaching to their tall hats long streamers of crape which reached to their heels, and bearing elaborate scrolls, the Inviters went from house to house reciting the virtues of the deceased and inviting his friends and relatives to attend the funeral. As they marched solemnly through the town, one tolled a bell, and the other struck his staff heavily against the ground, while he cried the tidings of death in a loud and doleful voice.

The Inviters to Funerals served as masters of ceremonies during the services, both at the home and at the cemetery. At the residence they met the guests and ushered them into the various rooms which had been set aside for the funeral reception. The parlor, which was seldom used except when a death occurred in the family, was reserved for intimate friends and near relatives. This gloomy chamber was furnished with heavy furniture, painted black, and a dozen or more high-backed chairs with rush bottoms, known as "dead chairs." They were used only at funerals, and none but mourners were permitted to sit in them. Prayers were said at the house, and then twelve friends of the deceased shouldered the coffin, which had been covered with a thick black cloth with heavy tassels, and carried it to the cemetery. The pall-bearers wore on their shoulders small white cushions, held in place by black bands across the back and chest. This was the origin of the pall-bearers' scarves, which are still worn in many parts of the United States.

After the coffin had been consigned to the grave, the Inviters to Funerals presented to each pall-bearer a spoon, the handle of which terminated in a crudely carved figure supposed to represent one of the Twelve Apostles. The resemblance was so poor, however, that they were commonly known as "monkey spoons," since the figure resembled a monkey more than it did an Apostle. Each of the female relatives of the deceased received from the Inviters, on behalf of the family, a mourning ring or a mourning brooch. The ring was inscribed with the age, name, and date of death of the late lamented, and the brooch contained a small lock of the deceased's hair. If he was bald, the hair of his closest male relative was substituted. The widow received a small piece of black velvet ribbon, which she publicly bound round her head in front of her cap, securing it in place with a mourning brooch. At some funerals gloves and scarves were distributed to every person in attendance.

When the services at the cemetery had been concluded, the relatives and friends of the deceased returned in solemn procession to the house, where they were served with cakes, spiced wine, and tobacco. They devoted the remainder of the day, and usually most of the night, to drinking and smoking. The liquor was invariably of the finest quality, for when a man married in colonial New York, one of the first things he did was to put aside a quantity of wine to be drunk at his funeral. It was not touched until that time arrived, so that sometimes the mourners were privileged to tickle their palates with fine old wine which had mellowed in casks for fifty years.

Some of early New York's funerals were as elaborate and extensive as the obsequies of a modern gang chieftain. The burial of a member of a prominent family never cost less than three thousand dollars, and quite often many times that amount. The funeral of the first wife of the Patroon Stephen Van Rensselaer, who owned much real estate in New York City and vast areas of land around Albany, cost twenty thousand dollars. Two thousand mourning scarves and an equal number of rings and brooches were distributed at the grave, and the pall-bearers' spoons were of solid gold. All of Van Rensselaer's tenants, several hundred in number, attended the funeral and were then entertained for four days at the manor house near Albany, all at the expense of the Patroon. The obsequies of Lucas Wyngaard, a bachelor and a man of considerable property, cost almost as much as those of Mrs. Van Rensselaer. During the afternoon and night after the funeral the mourners drank a pipe of wine, about two hundred and fifty gallons, and at dawn broke all the glasses and decanters and made a bonfire of their mourning scarves on the hearth. As further expression of their grief they also broke a few windows and added several pieces of furniture to the bonfire.

TRIVIA

THE ETIQUETTE of the calling card was rigidly observed in New York sixty or seventy years ago. The most fashionable card was large and square, engraved with the name of the person presenting it, and with appropriate words in the four corners. The corner containing the desired word was turned down to indicate the object of the call. Thus, in the upper right-hand corner was "felicitation," to be turned down on a visit of congratulation; on the lower left corner, "congé," for a visit just before leaving town; on the lower right, "condolence"; and on the upper left, "visite," for ordinary social calls.

Wedding invitations of this period contained the individual cards of the bride and groom, tied together with a white satin ribbon. Place-cards for private dinner parties were engraved with "Bon Appétit!" beneath which was lettered the name of the guest.

The phrase "bucket shop" was originally applied in New York to the cheap liquor stores of Baxter and other lower East Side streets, where wine, whisky, and beer were sold in small buckets by the pint, quart, or gallon.

■

The fattest Chinaman that ever lived in New York's Chinatown was probably Dang Fey, who owned a shop at No. 19 Pell Street during the late eighteen-nineties. He tipped the scales at 310 pounds. He was also famous in Chinatown for his ability to sleep. He often slumbered for three days without awaking, but always alone, for while asleep he kept up a continuous rolling motion from one side of the bed to the other.

■

"The question, 'will lager beer intoxicate?' first arose on this island," wrote a disgruntled author, Junius Henri Browne, in 1868, "and very naturally, too, considering the quality of the manufactured article. I have sometimes wondered, however, that there could be any question about it, so inferior in every respect is the beer made and sold in the metropolis. It is undoubtedly the worst in the United States—weak, insipid, unwholesome, and unpalatable; but incapable of intoxication, I should judge, even if a man could hold enough of it to float the Dunderberg [a famous iron-clad of the period]. It is impossible to get a good glass of beer in New York, and persons who have not drank it in the West have no idea what poor stuff is here called by the name."

■

The first white girl born in the colony of which Manhattan Island was a part was Sarah Rapaelje, daughter of Jan Joris and Catelina Trico Rapaelje. She was born on June 9, 1625, at Fort Orange, now a part of Albany. A year or so later her family removed to New York and built a house on Walleboght Bay, which the English corrupted into Wallabout. The bay was also known as the Bay of the Foreigners, because the country around it was settled by Walloons.

■

The pioneer resident of New York's Chinatown was Quimbo Appo, who came here about 1850 as a cook on the steamship *Valencia*. He married a white woman, but cut her throat a year or so later and was sentenced to be hanged. He obtained a new trial, was convicted of murder in the second degree, and served seven years in Sing Sing. About a year after his release he killed a Polish workman, for which he went to prison for five years. Then he married an Irish woman with a cork leg, who was known as Cork Maggie, and by her had a son, George Appo, who became notorious as a sneak-thief and pickpocket. Quimbo was soon sent to prison for stabbing Cork Maggie, and in 1875 was again sentenced for murdering another woman. He was finally transferred to the State Hospital for the Insane at Matteawan, where he died.

■

The first and probably the only money corner in the history of New York was engineered about 1665 by Frederick Phillipse, who lived in a small house behind the wall which the Dutch had erected along the present line of Wall Street. Wampum was the general medium of exchange in the colony, and by purchasing several hogsheads of the money from the Indians Phillipse created an artificial shortage of legal tender, so that whoever had contracted to pay for merchandise in wampum was compelled to buy from him at a high rate.

■

A great craze for yellow kid gloves struck the male population of New York during the late eighteen-sixties. Every man and youth who made any pretensions to style wore them, the yellower the better. They were regarded as such a necessary adjunct to the wardrobe of the well-dressed man that the city authorities appropriated enough money to buy a pair for every member of the City Council.

■

In colonial times a depression followed the present line of Maiden Lane from Nassau Street to the East River, and through it ran a brook over a clear, pebbly bottom. On the south the bank was steep, but on the north the slope was gentle and covered with grass. There the young Dutch women washed and bleached their linens, and because of this the settlers called it Maagde Paetje, or the Virgin's Path. Hence, Maiden Lane.

■

The first steamboat in America was sailed by John Fitch in the summer of 1796 upon the waters of the Collect, a large fresh-water pond which once occupied the present site of the Tombs and the Criminal Courts Building, eleven years before Robert Fulton sailed the Clermont up the Hudson River.

Fitch's ship was an eighteen-foot yawl, and was fitted with a screw propeller. The boiler was a twelve-gallon iron pot. Under the guidance of Fitch the craft circled the pond several times at the rate of six miles an hour.

■

The first permanent settlement along the present line of the Bowery was made about 1645 by ten Negroes and their wives, all superannuated slaves who had been given their freedom. They built cabins, and a stockade for cattle and protection against the Indians, on the present site of Chatham Square. Each of the Negroes agreed that his children were to remain slaves, and bound himself to pay to the city one fat hog and twenty-two and one-half bushels of grain annually.

■

Buttermilk Channel is now a deep arm of the sea between Governors Island and Red Hook, on the Brooklyn shore, but in early colonial times it was a narrow, shallow ford, easily crossed by cattle at low tide. The Indians and the Dutch settlers often waded from one shore to the other, and there is an authentic record of a little girl having been ferried over the channel in a wash-tub by an Indian squaw. Governors Island was originally called Nut Island, because of the great abundance of hickory, chestnut, and oak trees.

■

The Negro was introduced into New York in 1625 or 1626, when a ship arrived with eleven black men in the crew. They were immediately sold as slaves. Two years later three Negro women were brought to the colony. The first slave-ship docked in the harbor in June 1646, and the cargo of Negroes was traded for pork and peas. The Dutch colonists also enslaved Indians whenever the opportunity offered, but compared to the Negroes the number of Indian slaves was not large.

■

The first hotel, or tavern, in New York, was erected by the West India Company late in 1642 on the present site of No. 71–73 Pearl Street. In February 1643 it was leased to Philip Gerritsen, the first landlord, who paid an annual rental of about a hundred and twenty dollars. The tavern was used principally for the accommodation of English ship captains who stopped at New York on their way to and from New England. The building was used as a place of public entertainment until 1653, when it became the Stadt Huys, or City Hall.

■

A sovereign remedy for almost any physical ailment in New York during the middle of the seventeenth century was a concoction of calomel, sugar of lead, and pulverized human bones. Another medicine, especially recommended as an unguent for hypochondriacs, was the famous Balsam of Bats, invented by Sir Theodore Mayerne, physician to King Henry IV of France and to King Louis XIII. This was a rubbing-salve composed of adders, bats, sucking whelps, earthworms, and the marrow of the thigh bone of an ox.

■

Adam Roelantsen, the first school-teacher in New York, was sued in 1646 by a ship captain, who alleged that he had refused to pay passage money for a voyage from Holland to New York. The pedagogue contended that he owed the captain nothing, as he had said the ship's prayer throughout the voyage. The suit was thrown out of court when the captain admitted that Roelantsen had daily implored the Lord to protect and bless the ship and its crew, and admitted further that without these prayers the vessel would probably have been wrecked.

■

Backgammon was a favorite pastime of the unregenerate element of New York's early population and was popular for many years. Said one Alexander Mackraby in a letter dated June 13, 1678 and addressed to a friend in England: "They have a vile practice here, which is peculiar to the city; I mean that of playing at backgammon, which is going forward in the public houses from morning till night, frequently a dozen tables at a time." The game was confined almost entirely to the taverns, the good burghers refusing to permit such worldly diversions in their homes. This was true also of chess, checkers, and dominoes, while participation in a game of billiards was regarded as an infallible sign of depravity. Cards were played occasionally by the Dutch with a German pack of seventy-three cards, containing a king, a knave, a cavalier, and another face-card called the knecht, or hired man, but no queen. The pips were acorns, leaves, and hearts.

■

Mrs. Winslow's Soothing Syrup, which found its way down the throat of practically every American child some fifty years ago, was first manufactured in a house in East Broadway near Chatham Square. A restaurant occupied the ground floor of the building, and above a show window filled with food was perched the wooden effigy of an infant clutching a bottle.

■

The Borough of the Bronx derived its name from Jonas Bronck, an early Dutch settler who in 1636 purchased from the Indians a large tract of land between the Harlem and the Bronx Rivers.

■

Tight lacing was much in vogue among the fashionable women of New York around 1800, and the stays of the corsets in which they imprisoned themselves were constructed of steel or iron bands from two to four inches broad and from ten to eighteen inches in length. A popular ornament of this period was a golden heart suspended from a gold neckchain. The heart opened with a patent spring, and inside was a painting of the eye of a husband or a lover, executed on ivory and bordered with enamel.

■

The Church of the Transfiguration, on East Twenty-ninth Street near Fifth Avenue, was first called "The Little Church Around the Corner" in 1871. Joseph Jefferson went to a large church in Madison Avenue to arrange for the funeral of George Holland, an actor, but the minister said that he would not hold services over the body of anyone connected with the theater. He suggested that Jefferson ask the rector of "that little church around the corner."

■

The modern Tuxedo, or dinner-coat, first appeared in New York during the early eighteen-nineties and was first worn in the dance-halls and other resorts of the lower East Side. It was unknown in polite society for at least half a dozen years thereafter. The gay bloods of the Bowery and points east wore it in conjunction with white satin ties, white satin waistcoats, embroidered shirts, and diamond studs. It was called Tuxedo because it was offered for sale in the East Side shops and tailoring establishments about the time that the exclusive residential society of that name was founded by Pierre Lorillard. For several years the garment was also known as the Newport.

■

For some twenty-five years after the opening of Central Park, in the early eighteen-sixties, it was closed each evening at nine P.M. unless there was skating on the lakes, when visitors were permitted to remain until eleven. Entrance to the park was through eighteen gates—seven on Fifth Avenue, two at Sixth Avenue, two at Seventh Avenue, and seven on Eighth Avenue (now Central Park West)—at each of which was a sentry-box with a policeman always on duty. During the middle eighteen-eighties the park was so overrun by stray cats that a special force of men armed with rifles was employed to exterminate them.

■

A young man named Tatum, having imbibed too freely during a round of calls on New Year's Day 1786, fell into a snowdrift and went to sleep. When found next morning, he was dead. The Coroner's verdict was: "That the said Tatum's death was occasioned by the freezing of a large quantity of water in his body, that had been mixed with the rum he drank."

■

The roller-skating craze struck New York about the middle

of 1884, and within a few years there were almost as many roller-skating rinks in the city as there are motion-picture houses today. The first was the Cosmopolitan Rink, on the west side of the Broadway Theater, where Lew Wallace's *Ben Hur* was first produced. Throughout the eighteen-eighties and much of the nineties roller-skating was the principal pastime of citizens of every age and condition—business men went to work on skates, and skating parties were much in vogue among the fashionables. Several leading citizens and public officials seriously advocated equipping the police force with roller-skates, contending that a patrolman could then easily overtake a criminal.

■

One of the greatest attractions of the New York of the eighteen-eighties was the Time Ball on the roof of the Western Union Building in Broadway below Ann Street. Promptly at noon each day the Time Ball dropped from the top of a tall flagstaff, and hundreds of men lined the sidewalks, watch in hand, to get the correct time.

■

No man was considered well dressed in New York sixty years ago unless he possessed his own personal toothpick, which he carried in his vest pocket or wore as a watch-charm. These curious instruments, now almost obsolete, were made of quills. The picking end was sharpened, and the other was often plated with gold or silver, handsomely engraved, and sometimes encrusted with precious stones. Jewelers displayed them in their show windows at prices ranging from fifty cents to a thousand dollars.

■

Wall Street received its name from a wall, or palisade, which was erected across Manhattan Island along the line of thoroughfare in 1653, when the Dutch colonists expected an attack from the English. The posts were from twelve to fourteen feet high and seven inches thick. On the outside they were covered with boards, and inside a ditch three feet deep and two feet wide was dug. The dirt thus obtained was thrown against the wall, forming a platform high enough to enable the defenders of the settlement to look over the fortifications. Within fifty years the wall had fallen into disrepair, and in 1745 another one of palisades was built from about where No. 57 Cherry Street now stands across the island to the North River. It was constructed of cedar logs, with loop-holes for musketry, and a breastwork behind them. At intervals were blockhouses, with port-holes for cannon.

■

The first white owner of the present site of Yonkers was Adriaen Van der Donck, a lawyer. In Holland the son of a gentleman was called Jonkheer, and Van der Donck was known as Jonkheer Van der Donck. The English called the tract "The Jonkheer's land," and since the Dutch "j" is pronounced "y," the transition to Yonkers was soon accomplished.

■

Al Capone was not the first criminal in America to bear the nickname of Scar Face, at least so far as New York is concerned. The original owner of the appellation in the metropolis was a Chinaman, Charley Tong Sing, better known as Scar

Face Charley. He was so called because of a five-inch scar running diagonally across his face, which he had received during the Arctic voyage of the *Jeanette*, on which he was steward. During the late eighteen-nineties Scar Face Charley was head of the Hip Sing Tong, and was probably as efficient a highbinder as the New York tong wars ever produced. He served several prison terms and according to the police records of the period was responsible for at least six murders.

■

The first greenhouse on Manhattan Island was part of the pretentious establishment of James Beekman, whose mansion on a height at East River and Fifty-first Street was one of the show places of early New York. Lemon trees flourished under the glass roof of the greenhouse, and in 1776 George Washington picked with his own hands several lemons, which were made into lemonade in his presence. It was in the Beekman greenhouse that Nathan Hale was tried before Lord Howe of the British Army on the charge of being an American spy, and from it he was led forth to execution on September 21, 1776. He was hanged at what is now the northwest corner of Third Avenue and Sixty-sixth Street.

■

The cornerstone of the present City Hall, which is considered one of the finest examples of American architecture, was laid in 1803 by Mayor Edward Livingstone, and the building was completed and ready for occupancy in 1812. Exclusive of the furnishings, it cost $538,734. The front and side walls are of white marble quarried near Stockbridge, Massachusetts, but the rear wall is of domestic brownstone. The plans of the architect called for white marble throughout, but he was overruled by the Board of Supervisors, which decided that brownstone was good enough because the building was so far uptown that no one would ever see the rear wall anyway. The Supervisors officially expressed the opinion that New York would never extend beyond the northern limits of City Hall Park, and that the new structure would "not attract much notice from the scattered inhabitants who might reside above Chambers Street."

■

Curious records established in old New York: On April 16–17, 1878 Professor Cartier waltzed sixteen consecutive hours at Tammany Hall. On December 22, 1885 Frank Barrett opened 2,500 oysters in two hours, twenty-three minutes, thirty-nine and three-fourths seconds. In January and February 1883 W. S. Walcott ate two quails a day, between four and five o'clock in the afternoon, for thirty consecutive days. In April 1884 Charles Pearsall ate sixty soft-boiled eggs daily—thirty in the morning and thirty in the afternoon—for six consecutive days; and during the same month, a little farther north, at Tonawanda, New York, J. Baker ate six pounds of cooked beans in forty minutes.

■

New York's first nickname was The Flour City, bestowed upon it because during the last half of the seventeenth century the city had the exclusive right among the English colonies to bolt and pack flour and meal, and to manufacture bread for transportation. For many years two-thirds of the population was engaged in these occupations, and produced a grade of flour that had preference in all foreign markets. The metropolis was first called Gotham by Washington Irving in 1807, in "Chronicles of the Renowned and Ancient City of Gotham," one of the *Salmagundi* papers.

■

It was illegal to sell intoxicants to the Indians during the early years of the Dutch occupation, and if a savage was found drunk in the street without knowing at which house he had obtained the liquor, all the residents of the thoroughfare were liable to heavy fines.

■

The Jews of New York petitioned the Common Council in 1684 for permission to worship God in their own way, but were told by the Councillors that "no publique worship is tolerated but to those that profess faithe in Christ, and therefore the Jewish worship is not to be allowed."

■

Bowling Green, at the southern end of Broadway, was not the playground of the Dutch, but was established by three Englishmen—John Chambers, John Jay, and Peter Bayard. They leased the ground from the city in March 1732, enclosed it with a fence, and prepared it for the game of bowls, paying as rent one peppercorn a year. Their lease expired after eleven years, and Chambers, John Roosevelt, and Colonel Phillipse leased the enclosure for a similar period, paying twenty shillings a year. Originally the site was occupied by the city's first meat market, known as the Broadway Shambles, which was opened in 1658.

■

Women couldn't vote in early New York, but they were

occasionally permitted to hold minor public offices. In 1710 the widow of Andreas Donn became Public Scavenger of Broad Street, and a year later Rebecca Van Schaick, also a widow, was appointed to the post of Pound-Keeper. During the first hundred years of the city's existence the sale of fresh vegetables was almost entirely in the hands of women.

■

The first sparrows ever seen in New York, fourteen in number, were imported from Europe in 1863 and loosed in Central Park. They soon became numerous and were so popular that elaborate bird-houses in the form of Chinese pagodas were built for them in Union Square and other parks. Many citizens also kept them in their homes as pets.

■

The municipal hangman, Ben Johnson, was convicted of various thefts in 1672 and was sentenced to death, robbery at that time being a capital offense. The court ordered him to hang himself, but he refused to do so and contended that no one else could legally perform his duties. After much cogitation the judges reduced his punishment to thirty-nine lashes at the whipping-post, loss of an ear, and banishment from the colony, all of which was considered very mild.

■

In colonial times the largest and most delicious watermelons to be found in North America grew on Manhattan Island. One weighing forty-seven pounds was exhibited at Governor Sir George Clinton's residence in September 1750, and at the same time a New York merchant offered for sale a melon weighing forty-two pounds.

■

An extraordinarily large number of sharks infested the waters around the Catherine Slip Market during the first twenty years of the nineteenth century, and several men were employed by the butchers and fish-dealers to catch them from the dock. The best-known and most successful of the shark-catchers was an old man named Sam Way, who often caught as many as seven in one day, some of them fourteen feet and longer.

■

Bull-baiting, a popular sport in early New York, was introduced in 1763, when dogs worried a bull at the Delancey Arms tavern in the Bowery. The sport reached its zenith about 1800, when Samuel Winship, a butcher, built a bull-baiting arena on Bunker Hill, a hundred-foot elevation north of the present line of Grand Street, near Mulberry, where the Americans had constructed a fort during the Revolution. Winship enclosed the arena with a high board fence and erected seats for two thousand persons, each of whom paid twenty-five cents admission. The bull (and sometimes a bear or a bison) was chained to a large swivel ring set into the ground, with enough chain to permit the animal to run about in a large circle. Bull-dogs were then loosed against him.

■

Arthur Tappan, a wealthy silk merchant who with his brother Lewis founded the American Tract Society and the *Journal of Commerce*, promulgated, about 1825, the following rules of conduct for his many employees: Total abstinence; not to visit a theater or make the acquaintance of an actor; not to remain out after ten o'clock at night; not to visit bar-rooms or other wicked places; to attend prayer meetings twice a week; to belong to an anti-slavery society; to attend church service twice on Sundays, and on each Monday morning to submit a written report of the attendance, the name of the preacher, and the text of his sermon. Tappan is said to have advocated the use of the Army and Navy to compel his fellow-citizens to attend church. He once offered a million dollars for a small Hoboken park, where clerks and small tradesmen gathered to play games and drink beer, so that he could close it on Sundays.

■

The first New York City Directory was published in 1786 by David Franks. It contained 851 names, among them seven Smiths, one Kelly, and one Brown, but no Cohens. One stock-broker was listed—Archibald Blair, who on January 9 of that year announced that he had opened "a Broker's office and Commission store at 16 Little Queen Street, where he buys and sells all kinds of public and state securities, also old continental money. He has for sale Jamaica Rum, loaf sugar, bar iron, lumber and dry goods."

■

The first person to bring a breach of promise action in New York was Sergeant Peter Cock, who owned a tavern on the present site of No. 1 Broadway. In 1653 he sued Annetje Cornellisen Van Vorst, alleging that her promise to marry him was a valid and binding contract. After much litigation the Dutch courts decided in the Sergeant's favor, but the lady did not, after all, become his bride, although the old records fail to disclose the reason. Instead, she married his rival, a tobacco-planter.

■

A familiar and striking figure on the streets and in the taverns of New York during the latter part of the seventeenth century was Captain Thomas Tew, the notorious pirate, who was as bloodthirsty a villain as ever scourged the seas. Tew was then about forty years old, slightly built, and of such dark complexion that he was commonly believed to be part Negro. He usually wore a blue cap banded with cloth of silver; a blue jacket with gold lace borders and large pearl buttons; loose, knee-length white linen trunks; bright-colored stockings; and black slippers with massive gold buttons. A golden chain hung around his throat, and in his belt was a long dagger, its hilt encrusted with rubies, emeralds, diamonds, and other precious stones. This swaggering cut-throat killed at least three men in tavern brawls during his residence in New York, but he escaped punishment because of his friendship with Governor Benjamin Fletcher, to whom he gave rich presents of gold and jewels which had been stolen from merchant ships.

■

The first exhibition of Thomas Nast's cartoons was held in the back room of a saloon at Broadway and Twenty-second Street, which was opened in 1865 by Professor Jerry Thomas, inventor of the Tom and Jerry and the Blue Blazer, and the most illustrious bar-tender in the history of the metropolis. Professor Thomas also exhibited the work of Theodore Wust, Ned Mullin, and other popular artists of the period. After a few years, however, he abandoned art and began to collect gourds, with which he decorated the walls of his bar-room.

When he died, he owned more than a hundred of these use-
ful and ornamental vegetables.

■

Roger Baker, landlord of the King's Head Tavern, was placed
on trial in 1702 before Judge Atwood on a charge of treason,
it being alleged that he had publicly expressed the opinion
that the nose of the English King was constructed of wax.
One witness testified that he had heard Baker make the statement, but several others declared that they had been present
and had heard nothing of the sort. The jury promptly
returned a verdict of not guilty, whereupon Judge Atwood
angrily ordered them to deliberate again and to find Baker
guilty. Three times the jury reported not guilty, and just as
often the court refused to accept the verdict. The jurymen
were finally told that unless they convicted Baker they would
be whipped, branded with hot irons, and imprisoned. Without leaving the jury box they then decided that Baker was
guilty, and he was fined four hundred pieces of eight.

■

The most popular beverages in New York during the first half
of the eighteenth century were New England rum, commonly
called "kill devil," and applejack, which was produced in
large quantities in New Jersey and even then was known as
"Jersey lightning." Rum sold for as low as twenty-five cents
a gallon, but applejack was a little more expensive. No one
was expected to be strictly sober in the New York of that
period, and servants least of all. The prevailing attitude was
that of the citizen who in 1769 advertised for "an hostler that
gets drunk no more than twelve times a year."

■

Anthelme Brillat-Savarin, the celebrated French culinary expert, spent two years in New York, from 1794 to 1796, teaching French and playing in a theater orchestra. He invariably ate his dinner at Michael Little's Porter House at 56 Pine Street, which he described as the best eating-place in America. Brillat-Savarin and two other Frenchmen once met three Englishmen in a drinking bout at Little's tavern and drank the Englishmen under the table. They consumed, among other things, a bowl of punch sufficient for forty ordinary people.

■

The first white man killed in New York was John Coleman, an Englishman and a petty officer of the *Half-Moon*, the ship in which Henry Hudson sailed up the river which bears his name. Returning to the *Half-Moon* late in the afternoon of September 6, 1609, after a voyage in a small boat through the Narrows to Newark Bay, Coleman and four men of the crew were attacked by a war party of Indians. The others escaped, but Coleman was killed by an arrow.

■

The first Quakers to arrive in New York were Robert Hodgson and two women, who came to the New World from England in 1658. The women preached in the streets the day they landed, and were promptly arrested, fined, imprisoned for several months, and then banished to Rhode Island. Hodgson went to Hempstead, on Long Island, but was arrested when he started to preach. He was brought to Manhattan Island and by order of Governor Pieter Stuyvesant was subjected to extraordinary punishment. He was first pinioned in a painful position for twenty-four hours. Then he was tied head downward to the tail of a cart and taken to a dungeon in the city prison. A few days later he was tried and sentenced to two years at hard labor, and next day he was chained to a wheelbarrow with a Negro slave. He refused to work and was given one hundred lashes with a tarred rope four inches thick. This was repeated each day for four days, and then he was locked in the dungeon for two days without food or drink. On the third day he was suspended from the ceiling by his hands, with a heavy log tied to his feet, and was given another hundred lashes. He was again so punished after two more days without bread or water. He still refused to work, and after a week of this sort of punishment Stuyvesant's sister prevailed upon the Governor to release him. But he was forbidden to preach, and it was almost fifty years before the Quakers obtained full liberty to worship.

■

The first race-course in New York was established at Hempstead, on Long Island, in the spring of 1665 by Governor Richard Nicolls, who commanded the English fleet which had captured Manhattan Island from the Dutch. The course was laid out on a tract of land sixteen miles long and four miles wide, and was called "Newmarket," after the famous English sporting field. Five and six furlong sprints were unknown in those days, and even a mile race was uncommon. Usually races were run in two to four heats of from two to five miles each. Trotting races were unknown until 1818, when Boston Blue raced against time on the Jamaica Turnpike. The first match race between trotters was in 1823, when Topgallant, a famous horse of the period, defeated Dragon over a twelve-mile course from Brooklyn to Jamaica. Topgallant's time was thirty-nine minutes.

■

One of the sights of New York during the middle years of the nineteenth century was the 150-horsepower engine which furnished power for the presses of almost every newspaper, magazine, and book-publishing house in the city. The engine, together with a smaller machine which relieved it during the periods of minimum load, was in the basement of a building in Spruce Street, between William and Nassau Streets. Connected with the engine were three-fourths of a mile of main shafting, and two miles of connecting shafting and belting. One of the belts was of India rubber, 120 feet long. One shaft ran across Frankfort Street into the press-rooms of the *Mail;* another crossed William Street to print three hundred thousand copies of the *New York Ledger* each week, and a third crossed Spruce and went over back fences and through alleys into Beekman and Ann Streets, and thence into the press-rooms of half a dozen establishments. In 1868 the total number of presses operated by the engine was 125.

■

New Year's Eve was just another night in the New York of seventy-five years ago, and its observance was confined to the churches and a few pious families, which held watch-night services and parties. New Year's Day, however, was celebrated with a gusto that is unmatched by anything the modern metropolis has to offer. Practically the whole city held open house, and from nine o'clock in the morning until midnight the streets were filled with unattached men hurrying from house to house. Those who could afford to do so hired a carriage and coachman for the day, at a cost of from forty to fifty dollars. Few women were to be seen, as it was not considered respectable for a lady to be abroad on New Year's Day. Each man was intent upon making as many calls as possible before he was overwhelmed by the enormous quantities of food and drink which were served at every house. The principal beverage was punch, most of which was prepared by professional punch-makers. Professional hairdressers, or "artistes in hair," as they called themselves in those elegant times, also reaped a harvest on New Year's Day. They were in such demand to construct the elaborate coiffures of the period that they began their rounds before midnight on December 31, and the ladies who were unfortunate enough to be among the first on their lists had to sit up for the remainder of the night, in order that their crowns of glory might not be tilted askew.

■

The most powerful man in New York society for some thirty years during the middle of the nineteenth century was Isaac H. Brown, owner of a lucrative undertaking business and sexton of Grace Episcopal Church, then the most fashionable congregation in the city. Brown was father confessor to the upper crust; he arranged funerals, weddings, receptions, and other functions, dictating the invitation lists and ruling with an iron hand. He did everything in an extraordinarily genteel manner. "The Lenten season is a horridly dull season," he once said, "but we manage to make our funerals as entertaining as possible." So far as New York is concerned, Brown appears to have foreseen the reign of the gigolo, for he had at his command—his enemies, who described him as a "fat old gabbler," said in his employ—a large number of elegant young men, whom he dressed in black swallow-tailed coats and dispatched as escorts for lonesome ladies, or to fill gaps at parties. In appearance the social director was huge and

beefy, with a red face and coarse features. His habitual costume included a long frock coat and a diamond stud as large
as a man's thumb, which gleamed from the bosom of a white
embroidered shirt.

INDEX